The
Book of Hay

The Book of Hay

by
Kate Clarke

Logaston Press

LOGASTON PRESS
Little Logaston Woonton Almeley
Herefordshire HR3 6QH

Published by Logaston Press 2000

ISBN 1 873827 61 X

Set in Times by Logaston Press
and printed in Great Britain by
MFP Design & Print, Manchester

Cover illustration from:
Hay-on-Wye by David Cox, 1783-1859

Contents

Acknowledgments

I should like to thank all those persons who have been willing to share their local knowledge—Mary Morgan, Olive Grainger, Gladys Southgate, Betty Jones, Bob Knights and his late wife Marina, David Lockwood, Ken and Violet Jenkins, Peter Fowler, Eric Pugh and Desmond Potter—and especially Sid Wilding and Nigel Birch whose attention to detail has been invaluable. Appreciation too for the assistance of the publisher, Andy Johnson, with regard to the early history of Hay and the Welsh Borders.

Thanks for illustrations are due to a number of people and organisations, to Brian Byron for the map on page 8; Bernard Grant for the photographs from the collection of the late John Grant on pages 6, 38, 39, 55, 60 (both), 61, 62 and 109; Eric Pugh for those on pages 21, 51, 52, 58, 63, 64, 70, 71 and 102; Adrian Gillard for that on page 15; Richard Booth for those on pages 26 and 110; Mr D.A. Price for that on page 32; the National Library of Wales for that on page 45; Mrs Mary Ridger for that on page 48; Brecknock Museum, Brecon for that on page 50; Frank Bennett for that on page 54; Mr Percy Price for that on page 59; Messrs T.A. Matthews for those on pages 76, 85 and 86; PopperFoto for that on page 100 and Logaston Press for those on pages 5, 7, 27, 33, 41, 56 and 104. Thanks are also due to Birmingham City Art Gallery for permission to use part of the painting by David Cox for the front cover. I should also like to thank Jonathan Cape for permission to quote from *The Diary of Rev Francis Kilvert*.

Introduction

There is, undeniably, something unique about Hay, though what makes it so special is difficult to define. Whatever it is, it attracts thousands of tourists from all over the world, many combining a passion for books with a love of the surrounding countryside which is surely some of the most beautiful in the country.

The people of Hay have become accustomed to a continual influx of bibliophiles fanatically searching for particular books, so obscure they are hard to find or simply out-of-print: the solemn-faced students, weighed down with the prospect of examinations too imminent for complacency; the elderly ladies happily rummaging through piles of books looking for that long-remembered title, or that gripping tale lent to a friend in 1945 and never returned. Whereas for some 'anything by Catherine Cookson' will suffice, for others only a first edition of their favourite author will do. Many a lone biker has beaten a path to Hay in search of a Harley Davidson manual, *circa* 1957, any condition; and in sharp contrast comes a gentle stream of pale pedantic vicars searching, perhaps, for inspirational tracts in dusty tomes long forgotten. And in their wake the steady flow of worshippers of Arthur Rackham, A.A. Milne and J.R. Tolkien, devotees of Biggles and those who have become quite irrational about Rupert Bear. Like rivers to the sea they all come to Hay where they can browse in peace, left to wallow in, literally, millions of out-of-print books.

Visitors to the town invariably ask the same questions—Why books? Why Hay? Who started it all? Is there really a king in the castle and, on different tacks, where did Major Armstrong, hanged for murder in 1922, live and work? How has the town survived on a fractious frontier down the centuries?

This book provides a brief history of Hay, intended to satisfy the curious visitor who has, perhaps, neither the time nor desire to plough through more weighty works on the history of the Marches.

This is, of course, simply one person's view of Hay. It goes without saying that a great many former residents not mentioned here, have contributed greatly to the prosperity of the town. Any brief history such as this must be, by the limited space available, selective and therefore subjective. Inevitably, it will fall to future writers, removed by the passage of time, to effectively chronicle the scores of people whose diverse skills are at present contributing to the health, wealth and security of the people of Hay. Only then, when both feuds and friendships are long forgotten, will it be possible to distinguish between those who, several generations hence, will have faded from, and those who will have remained clearly focused within, the collective memory of the town.

The story of Hay is one of a small town surviving Norman invasion, border fracas, rebel attacks and, more recently, the effects of the Industrial Revolution. It is now, like many small towns, suffering the onslaught of heavy articulated lorries trying to negotiate the narrow streets that were designed to accommodate the passage of people and animals, not vehicles.

In addition, one wonders whether Hay, despite having been designated as a Conservation area in 1969 and being part of the Brecon Beacons National Park, must suffer still further erosion of its magnificent landscape by the industrial development that is is creeping up on all sides, an onslaught of ugliness as damaging as any the town has suffered in the past. Hay is faced with a dilemma shared by many rural communities—the need to create employment opportunities to maintain its growth and prosperity without destroying the surrounding countryside in the process. Should the book-selling business become largely computerised with customers able to order virtually every available out-of-print book without leaving their home or office, the town of Hay may need to rely on the beauty of its setting to still attract visitors to the town. Sadly, the damage done by too much industrial development is irrevocable and could destroy forever the rural character of Hay and thereby rob it of two of its most valuable characteristics—its individuality and its charm.

CHAPTER 1

Hay Castle

The small market town of Hay lies at the foot of the Black Mountains, on the south bank of the River Wye. It stands on the border between England and Wales at a point where three old counties meet—Herefordshire to the east, Brecknockshire to the west and Radnorshire to the north, the latter two now part of Powys. This alignment has had a marked effect on the development of Hay and like many Marcher towns and villages it shares a special character forged by the equally strong Welsh and English influences, not least in the tolerant ambivalence of its people. (The word 'March' for the border, is derived from the Saxon *mearc*, meaning a border between two nations.)

In Neolithic times, the 'new stone' age, (*c.*4,000 - 2,500 BC) there is evidence for extensive human occupation of the ring of hills facing the Black Mountains. Prior to this period hunter gatherers had moved along the river valleys, spreading out into the hills on their hunting expeditions. Evidence for this comes in finds of flint flakes, where they sharpened the flints acquired through trading from tribes further afield into the arrow and spear heads needed in their hunting. As the population expanded and people learnt to domesticate stock and plant and harvest crops, people started to form permanent settlements. One has been excavated above Dorstone, at the head of the Golden Valley, and shows it to have been occupied by around 250 people. They would have been responsible for the construction of the nearby Arthur's Stone burial chamber, along with others in the vicinity. A total of six Neolithic occupation sites have been found in the vicinity of the Black Mountains, along with 18 tombs, including those at Ffoystyll north and south and Ty Isaf. Apart from the style of construction, these tombs share a common feature.

They're all built on the flanks of hills that face towards the Black Mountains, not on the hills' highest points. It's as if the Black Mountains were then the focus of people's existence.

In the Bronze Age, with better weather conditions, more use was made of the Black Mountains themselves, with some round barrows, the new style tomb, being built and the occasional small stone circle. Towards the end of the Bronze Age, larger settlements were created within hillforts, with farms in the valleys below. This was the age of Celtic Britain.

There is evidence of a pre-Roman community on the northern banks of the River Wye at Hay, and of a Roman camp nearby. Some 8 to 10 miles to the east of the town runs the ancient earthwork, Offa's Dyke, a defensive bank that marked the boundary between the territories of Celtic Cymru and Saxon Mercia, which followed on, in due course, from Roman Britain and subsequent Dark Ages. It was built by King Offa, who ruled the Saxon kingdom of Mercia between 757 and 796 AD. The present border between England and Wales meanders erratically through the Marches, sometimes to the east of the line of the Dyke, sometimes the west and rarely along it.

Offa's Dyke Path, opened in 1971, runs from Prestatyn in the north to Chepstow in the south, roughly following the route of Offa's Dyke in the northern and far southern sections, but where the dyke is more intermittent in the Hereford Plain, the path heads across country to the Black Mountains, along whose eastern flank it then runs. The reason for lack of evidence for the Dyke in Herefordshire is unclear. There are sections to the west of both Lyonshall and Weobley and near Byford. But once it meets the Wye all evidence vanishes. The generally accepted belief is that a semi-independent kingdom called Ergyng and later Archenfield, existed, sandwiched between the Wye and the Black Mountains, which guaranteed the frontier's security. Certainly something of the sort must have been in place, for it would be unusual to build a major city, Hereford, right on the frontier. The path was created by the National Parks Commission (now the Countryside Commission) and brings hundreds of walkers to Hay each year.

Hay itself starts to come of age with the arrival of the Normans, the name even deriving from the Norman La Haie, meaning a fenced or hedged enclosure; the Welsh name for Hay is Y Gelli—a grove or wood. William fitzOsbern was created Earl of Hereford by William I, and organised the construction of a line of major castles along the border in his sphere of influence. Some were constructed by barons to whom lands were granted, these lands becoming Marcher Lordships, semi-independent petty kingdoms, with many of their own local laws. Nominally held from the Crown, the king's only effective way to control these barons was to also grant them land within England itself, ensuring their presence on occasion closer to the seat of government. One perquisite of being a Marcher Lord, was that the baron could seek to conquer and then hold any land he chose from the Welsh.

Many Marcher manors, Hay included, were divided into English and Welsh sections. The manors of English Hay (*Hay Anglicana*) and Welsh Hay (*Haia Wallensis*) have no bearing on the present day boundaries between the two countries, which follow the course of the Dulas Brook, entering the Wye downstream from the bridge.

On the fall from grace of the fitzOsberns after the rebellion of William's heir, Roger, in 1075, the role of the leading Marcher in the area around Hay fell to Bernard Neufmarché. In 1093 he defeated the Welsh king, Rhys ap Tewdr of Deheubarth (based in south-west Wales) in a battle near Brecon, where he already appeared to be building a castle. Hay Castle had probably been commenced upon the early Norman encroachments from their original bases, in campaigns in the 1070s. No doubt it was further strengthened in the campaigns of 1093. Another, smaller castle site, of which nothing now remains but the mound, referred to locally as The Tump, situated close to the parish church, was built by another Norman baron, William Revel, at the end of the 12th century, in a landholding separate to that of Hay Castle.

The fact that Hay Castle was commenced soon after the Norman Conquest is attested by the cleric Giraldus Cambrensis. In 1188 he passed through Hay in the company of the Archbishop of Canterbury, who was on a mission to recruit men to join the second crusade, the aim of which was to repossess Jerusalem after its capture by Saladin in 1187. To this end Giraldus preached a sermon in front of the castle, a fortification which he implied in his writings was already well-established.

Castles such as these provided strongholds from which the local countryside was controlled and income derived, and in which alliances were made and invasions planned with great frequency, and which were marked by unbridled enthusiasm and thuggery on both sides. Rebellion, land grabbing and double-dealing were rife and a fighting man's allegiance was often transitory, switching from one war lord to another, even from one country to another, whenever it was expedient either for monetary gain, the acquisition of land or simply in order to survive.

When Bernard Neufmarché died in 1123 the castle at Hay passed to his daughter, Sybil, and her husband, Miles Gloucester. He was created Earl of

3

Hereford and became Constable of England, possessing lands in the counties of Hereford, Gloucester and also in Brecknock. He owned, but probably did not occupy, the castle at Hay for more than twenty years until he was killed, whilst hunting, with an arrow to the heart in 1143.

Hay Castle then passed down the family to Miles's daughter, Bertha, who was married to Philip, son of William Breos. Some twenty years later her eldest son, another William Breos, known as 'The Ogre', inherited the lordship of Hay and a definite penchant for violence, killing Prince Seisyll and other Welsh princes whilst they were guests at dinner in Abergavenny Castle. Through this and other bloody skirmishes he acquired castles in Radnor, Builth and Brecon, thereby wielding formidable power in the Marches, first during the reign of King Richard I and then, for a while at least, King John.

It was William 'The Ogre' who was married to Matilda St Valerie, sometimes known as Moll Walbee or Maud de Haia, whom legend has it was a giantess who, about 1200, replaced the old wooden castle with one made of stone in the space of a single day. It is more likely that she was simply a strapping young woman who happened to be significantly taller than the indigenous Welsh and therefore attributed with unusual strength. The story could, however, have arisen from events in 1198, when she was one of those responsible for first assembling at Hay and then leading an army which destroyed a large Welsh force then beseiging Painscastle. As for the sudden appearance of a stone castle at Hay, it may have been that the trees around the site were felled during the building, probably for use in constructing wooden scaffolding, suddenly revealing the new stone castle to people living in the surrounding hills, thereby adding fuel to the fantasy.

The castle at Hay was strategically placed on prominent high ground facing the River Wye. The community within the castle would have been completely self-sufficient with all that was necessary for the survival of men-at-arms—saddlers, blacksmiths, weavers, clerks and cooks—with the livestock conveniently housed and slaughtered within the curtilage of the castle.

Though the main function of the castle was military and administrative there would have been accommodation for a visiting war lord and his retinue—a great hall and solar, or upper room—in addition to the stables, storerooms and kitchens. In fact, everything necessary for an enclosed community at siege and, of course, dungeons into which sundry miscreants could be thrown when necessary.

According to legend, whilst Maud was building the castle she carried pebbles from the river in her apron and when one of them fell into her shoe

4

Hay Castle from the market square to its south, showing the entrance gateway and adjacent tower

she lost her temper and threw it across the River Wye. Her strength and the velocity of her throw was such that the small boulder landed in Llowes, a village more than two miles away! A stone called 'Maud's boulder', seven feet high, a foot wide and decorated with 7th and 11th century crosses, now rests inside St Meilig's Church at Llowes and the legend lives on. A stone effigy, badly deteriorated, reputed to be of Maud, lies in St Mary's Church in Hay, though it is thought more likely to be that of an unknown monk.

Whether Maud did, indeed, possess miraculous building skills we cannot know but there is no doubt about her propensity for careless talk and incurring large debts. In 1208, she and her husband had accrued huge debts owed to King John, and seemed loathe to repay them. With warfare going badly in Normandy and Wales, there were murmurings of discontent and John demanded hostages from those whose motives he found suspicious—including de Breos. When a minion was sent to fetch her sons as hostages, Maud had the audacity to refuse, saying: 'My boys I will not deliver to your King John because he basely slew his nephew, Arthur, whom it was his duty honourably to protect.' The latter had first claim to the throne and William Breos had witnessed his slaughter by the King's men and unwisely told his wife.

This refusal was an act of treason, and John acted swiftly, Maud and William fleeing to Ireland, presently pursued there by the King. Maud escaped to Scotland with her sons, but was eventually captured. Promising to repay her debts forthwith she pledged the castles of Hay and Radnor as security but as she and William subsequently defaulted on the payments their lands and property were seized by King John. As befits such reckless behaviour they both died miserably, as characters in a Dickensian melodrama—the wretched Maud and her eldest son were imprisoned, some say walled up alive, and starved to death in Windsor Castle in 1210; William, under self-imposed exile and in poverty in France the following year,

This brutal treatment of a powerful baron and his family instigated a furious backlash. The wrath of William's two brothers, Reginald and Giles, was such that, in 1215, they regained the castles of Brecon lordship, including that of Hay. Giles's part in this vengeful affray was a little surprising as he was Bishop of Hereford at the time. Later in the year the brothers forged an alliance with the most powerful Welsh prince, Llywelyn Fawr ab Iorwerth, Prince of Gwynedd, cementing relations with the marriage of Reginald to Llywelyn's daughter, Gwladys Ddu. This alliance was to have unusual consequences. In the meantime, in 1216, King John counterattacked and 'made for the Radnor and Hay and laid siege to them and overthrew the castles to the ground'.

In 1215, the year before he died, King John was forced to sign Magna Carta, a treaty between himself and the barons incorporating,

The castle gateway in the 1980s

6

amongst other things, the right to trial by a jury of one's peers. This weakened the untrammelled power of the monarch but was necessary to appease the barons and restore some semblance of peace, no matter how short-lived, to the borders.

Ten years later, Maud and 'The Ogre's' grandson, yet another William Breos, had become the owner of Hay Castle. It had been rebuilt by Reginald Breos but in 1229 he was caught romancing Llywelyn's wife, Joan, King John's natural daughter. To add to the insult he was supposed to be arranging his own daughter Isabella's marriage to Llywelyn's

The tower is the castle's earliest masonry structure, though large parts have been rebuilt either due to poor foundations or when the house was added

son, Dafydd, at the time. Moralists will note that he paid for his lust with his life, being hanged from a tree.

Henry III subsequently put Hay Castle into the hands of William Marshall, uncle of William's three daughters. On his death in 1231, the lordship passed to Hubert de Burgh, Justiciar of England. The 'rightful' ownership of much of Breconshire had become confused through warfare, rebellion, marriage and divisions of estates between heirs, that the contenders had to resort to further warfare to try to stake a physical claim. Llywelyn, laying claim through Isabella's marriage to Dafydd, struck in 1231, advancing across Breconshire, attacking Hay Castle and burning the town, and also winning a skirmish literally in the Wye near the town, when 300 English knights were said to have been killed.

Within a few years, however, the castle was once more repaired and sufficiently grand to accommodate a visit from the King himself. Perhaps in recompense for the death of her husband, William Breos's widow, Eva, was given the castle by the King as part of her dowager's estate. It was during her tenancy that the town walls were built for added protection against the attentions of marauding rebels from the west and, perhaps, against the packs of wolves that roamed the area. King Henry is reputed to have said that there were more wolves in the area north of Hay than anywhere else in his kingdom.

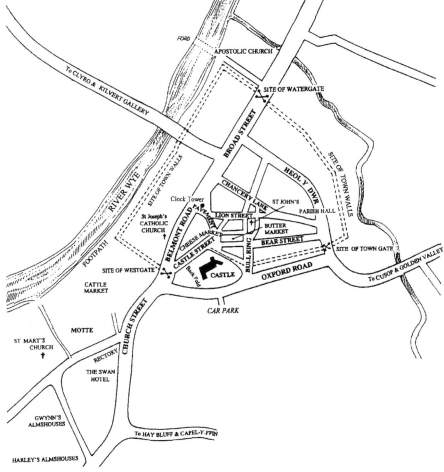

Plan of Hay showing the old walls and gates

In 1236, he gave Eva Breos a special charter allowing her to charge a 'murrage' toll once a week for three years to pay for the building of the town wall. The smaller motte and the original church, now St Mary's, both built before 1237, were actually outside the town wall. Only one or two small sections of this wall remain but the course it took is well documented.

There were three main gates to the town and a postern. The Watergate (Nyport) was in Newport Street by the Lamb Inn (now the premises of Coles' veterinary surgery) and close to the plaque in the wall opposite, marking the site of one of the town's wells. The west or Carlesgate was in Church Street, close to the junction of Castle Street and Belmont Road which led to the two main thoroughfares—one being the route leading from Belmont Road down the length of Broad Street to Watergate and thence to Clifford. The other thoroughfare passed along Castle Street to the area originally used as a market place including the Bull Ring, Castle Lane, St John's Place and High Town. The exact position of Black Lion Gate is not known but it was probably near the Old Black Lion Inn at the bottom of Bear Street and from there leading to Hardwick Road.

The other means of approaching the town would have been either by the ferries of which there were two, or, when the river was sufficiently low, and in order to avoid the payment of tolls, by crossing the ford near Water Gate. It must be said however, that on account of the fast-flowing currents crossing by either method must have been extremely hazardous.

Although for several years exposed to attack from Llywelyn's forces Hay appears to have remained unscathed during this period. A truce arranged in 1234, followed by Llywelyn Fawr ab Iorwerth's death in 1240, brought comparative peace. Indeed, the next threats came from within England in the late 1250s and early 1260s as concerns over Henry III's rule moved from gestures and attempts at control through parliament into civil war. In 1264, Henry and his son, Prince Edward, were taken prisoner by Simon de Montfort, leader of a reformist baronial party, at the Battle of Lewes in Sussex, and spent some time as prisoners in Hereford. De Montfort was forced to spend time on the borders, for one of the king's staunchest allies was Roger Mortimer, of Wigmore, from whose constable he took the surrender of Hay Castle. In due course, Edward escaped to join Mortimer and the various forces spent time manouevering around the Marches, In June 1265, Hay became the centre of affairs as de Montfort, his prisoner Henry III and Llywelyn ap Gruffyd (grandson of Llywelyn Fawr ab Iorweth) negotiated a treaty of alliance. With his rear secure, de Montfort moved to Evesham, defeat and death.

Warfare continued along the border, but with affairs being directed by the firmer hand of Prince Edward, the warfare receded westwards. Further peaceful times followed the death of Llywelyn, killed in a skirmish, in 1282. Hay Castle, meanwhile, passed to the de Bohuns in another division of property, a family set to retain control for nearly a hundred years.

CHAPTER 2

Hay in the Middle Ages

The 14th and 15th centuries were times of continuing lawlessness and border unrest. The castle was involved in the rebellion led by Owain Glyndwr in the early 1400s, but suffered little consequence from the later strife between the Lancastrians and Yorkists in the Wars of the Roses. Also, the town, being somewhat remote, managed to escape the terrors of the first two plague epidemics and although affected by the third outbreak in 1359, the losses were not as high as in many other places, causing minimal interference with the feudal system.

In other parts of the country, however, the Black Death did much to break down the system by depopulating vast areas of land, killing off peasants and ruling barons alike. This meant that, for the first time, land that became vacant was bought, not seized in battle or inherited by birth, bought, moreover, by those survivors who were enterprising enough to overcome the devastating toll on the workforce by abandoning the small arable holdings in favour of less labour intensive sheep farming. This led to a thriving wool industry in which Hay soon gained importance as one of the largest trading centres in the area.

Yet the feudal system in Hay changed little throughout the Middle Ages. The Lordship of the manor of Hay remained in the de Bohun family until 1373 when the last Humphrey de Bohun died. As his two daughters, Eleanor and Mary, were still minors, the castle reverted once more to the Crown.

During the time they had owned the castle the de Bohuns had done well out of the people of Hay, aided by many of Henry IV's harsh anti-Welsh laws which enabled them to maintain their power. In the Welsh section of Hay the customary tenants, working on pitifully small holdings, were subject to manifold dues. In addition to paying rent to the lord of the manor they also had to work his land for a certain number of days each year, although this could sometimes be waived on payment of a substantial annual sum.

There were few loop-holes for avoiding military service, however. Every able-bodied man was liable to be mustered, either to guard the castle or follow the lord of the manor and his supporters into battle. It was also obligatory for all tenants to attend the manorial courts even though this often incurred loss of wages. Failure to attend could result in a fine of 10 shillings, the equivalent of several weeks' wages.

Although, following the signing of Magna Carta, any inhabitant of Hay with a grievance—provided he was a free man—had some redress through the complex legal system, it is doubtful that any individual without means could have seriously challenged the interests of the lord of the manor and his deputies. These officials, the stewards and bailiffs, could earn as much as £20 a year, on top of any bribes they could muster. And they were, no doubt, adept at sorting out most everyday problems on the spot and with a degree of brutality. Indeed, many of the cases that came before the courts were complaints lodged against these official bully-boys but they were, in effect, answerable only to the lord of the manor and in many instances they clearly ruled by fear.

In many ways the feudal system was a form of slavery for a customary tenant and his family were considered to be the property of the manorial lord. A fine of 4 shillings, for instance, was levied against a man if his daughter married or was unchaste. Further restrictions prevailed over every aspect of a tenant's life. Failure to take advantage of the lord's communal facilities, for which he charged a fee, would also incur a fine. In this way he held a monopoly on a number of daily activities such as grinding corn, washing clothes, baking bread and even the slaughter of animals.

The manorial lord was also in receipt of all gate tolls, rents from market stalls and ferries in addition to the tolls and other revenue from the fairs which were held regularly in Hay. These were supervised by the constable—he was also in charge of the castle—who must have been tempted to supplement his relatively low income of £5 a year by accepting bribes.

The roads around Hay at this time would have been little more than rough drovers' tracks between small, isolated communities and many would have been impassable in winter. They were also plagued by groups of bandits who would lay in wait for vulnerable wayfarers, making the simplest journey a risky venture. Drovers, having walked their livestock to the meat markets of the Midlands or even London, were especially vulnerable to attack on their way home carrying the income from their sales. The remote and treacherous road over the mountains to Capel-y-ffin, known as Gospel Pass, for instance, was notoriously dangerous for those travelling alone or in small groups. If the highway robbers failed to get their hands on the money, the landlords of the drovers' pubs were waiting to take their share.

However, in 1285, a law was passed whereby the roads were to be extensively widened and all trees and bushes removed within two hundred feet, the length of an arrow shot, on either side. It was hoped that this would break the cover of bandits and allow travellers to pass unmolested. These safety measures were fairly successful and led to a steady increase in the amount of travel in the 14th century.

There were, of course, a great many people making annual pilgrimages to the numerous holy places within Wales, the excessively devout stopping to kiss religious relics—the supposed ears, toes or skulls of various saints—on the way. Having a vested interest in keeping up this lucrative religious fervour the churches and monasteries contributed to the maintenance of the roads.

In addition to the pilgrims and drovers there were large numbers of tramps, beggars and casual labourers constantly on the move. As the system of serfdom slowly broke down more men and women, previously tied to the lord of the manor and the locality in which they lived, were free to wander in search of work that paid the highest wages. In response, Government tried to fix wages by statute, and also prevent such movement of people, in 1495 issuing a Vagrancy Act which ordered that all 'vagaboundes, idell and suspecte persons lyving suspeciously' should be put in the stocks for three days, fed only on bread and water and then expelled from the town or village.

The roads were also used by common carriers who would convey goods at a charge of a penny per ton for each mile covered. They used strings of pack-horses, sometimes as many as fifty, equipped with wicker panniers at their sides. Men of means would travel on horse-back and the horse litter for ladies was still commonly used, but for the majority of people in the Hay area travel was on foot or on the back of a farm cart.

Not only was there a glaring discrepancy in the quality of life between lord and tenant there was also gross ethnic inequality between the inhabitants of Welsh and English Hay. All positions of authority—those of sheriff, bailiff or steward—were invariably held by Englishmen which, in turn, led to prejudice and corruption. The system was patently unfair and resentment amongst the Welsh culminated in the rise of the legendary Owain Glyndwr. Owain took advantage of a power vacuum created by the machinations of Richard II and subsequent usurpation of the throne by Henry IV, and early successes in a guerrilla style war soon brought him many adherents, notably in north Wales, his home territory.

As ineffective measures were taken against the uprising—Henry's reign was bedevilled by an almost bankrupt treasury and constant warfare along the borders of his kingdom—the uprising turned to open rebellion and those from central and south Wales, including several Englishmen, joined with Owain. The borders of both Shropshire and Herefordshire were under threat of constant raids.

It is difficult to ascertain the extent of local support for Owain Glyndwr. It may be that the people of Hay were less antagonistic towards the English than those from further north and west. There had been, after all, a certain amount of intermarriage between the nations, including the local nobility, either for love, security or social status. The intermarriage between the de Breoses and the family of Llywelyn Fawr ab Iorwerth of Gwynedd has been noted; the scholar, Giraldus Cambrensis, who accompanied Archbishop Baldwin, was himself, as he noted, 'sprung from the Prince of Wales and from the Barons of the Marches' to which he added, 'when I see injustice in either race, I hate it.'

Undoubtedly, these and many other intermarriages did much to create a more tolerant attitude and recruitment to the rebel cause may well have been slow in border areas like Hay, areas which also lay closer to the centres of English power.

In 1402, Owain Glyndwr defeated the English in the battle of Pilleth, near Presteigne, where, incidentally, it is said that Welsh women stormed onto the battlefield armed with knives to mutilate the enemy. One of those captured was Sir Edmund Mortimer, a Marcher lord who turned out to be sympathetic to the rebel cause. Furthermore, far from being intimidated by the rampaging Welsh viragos he eventually married Jane, one of Glyndwr's seven daughters. Four years later he was to show remarkable courage when besieged by King Henry's men at Aberystwyth Castle, for he starved to death protecting his family.

As for Hay Castle it came under attack fairly regularly during these troubled times and was severely damaged by marauding rebels from the north. Clifford Castle, home of the legendary Jane Clifford, mistress of Henry II, later to be immortalised as 'fair Rosamund' in Tennyson's 'A Dream of Fair Women', was destroyed. Throughout most of 1404 Hay Castle was under the command of Sir John Oldcastle, from Herefordshire, one of the rising military stars gathering around the leadership of Prince Henry, the future Henry V. However, Oldcastle is remembered in history as a leading Lollard, who was subsequently hung, drawn and quartered on the authority of his old friend, the Prince; and in mythology as Sir John Falstaff in Shakespeare—Shakespeare's early drafts refer to Sir John Oldcastle.

Under Prince Henry and his captains, the English developed new tactics, of mounting and combining flying columns from the castle garrisons to counter attack the enemy. In 1405 a total of 140 men were drawn from both

Humphrey de Bohun (left) and Edward Stafford,
Duke of Buckingham (right), from a window in Brecon Cathedral

the English and Welsh parts of Hay for the 'defence and safe keeping of the town of Hay for 14 days and nights against rebels advancing from Radnorshire'; in April the garrison was given as 16 men-at-arms and 80 archers, some of whom subsequently served in the new attacking tactics.

These soon bore fruit and south and central Wales returned to English control, west and north Wales largely succumbing over the next couple of years. The people were war weary and it was their disinterest in continuing strife, coupled with the English resurgence, which helped to end the fighting.

In 1413, King Henry IV died and was succeeded by his son, veteran of the Owain campaigns. Owain was still at liberty, and Henry offered him a pardon if he would accept English sovereignty. He refused. The fate of the rebel leader is unknown. One story has him drifting into a peaceful old age in the home of one of his daughters in Herefordshire. Another, that he died from exhaustion on one of the Welsh mountains he so dearly loved.

Hay Castle passed into the hands of the dukes of Buckingham through a series of heiresses. In 1460, early in the Wars of the Roses, Humphrey Stafford, the first duke of Buckingham, was killed in the battle of Northampton. When an inventory of his assets was made the castle at Hay was described as 'ruinous, destroyed by rebels and of no value'. His young grandson, Henry Stafford, became the second duke of Buckingham and grew to be an arrogant and ambitious man with a reputation for brutality. He supported Richard III's claim to the throne, became one of his greatest allies and possibly the most powerful baron in the country. Besides Hay he owned vast estates and bore the title of Governor of all the King's castles in Wales and Steward to all the royal manors in Shropshire and Herefordshire. And, to add to his phenomenal power, he was also Chief Justice and Chamberlain of Wales and Lord High Constable of England. In a recent *Sunday Times* survey he was named the 17th richest person in British history with an estimated fortune of the equivalent of £14.4 billion in today's currency. His downfall came, however, when his ambition led him to support Henry Tudor's claim to the throne. Gathering an army at Brecon, he advanced eastwards, but finding the Severn valley blocked by floods, retreated to Weobley in Herefordshire, his forces disintegrating around him. Richard took Buckingham hostage and ordered his execution for Treason, without trial, at Salisbury in 1483.

As his son, Edward Stafford, the third duke of Buckingham, was only seven when he inherited his father's estates they passed into the custody of Thomas Vaughan, on behalf of the Crown. Two years later, in 1485, young Henry Tudor, back in England after an exile of 14 years, defeated Richard at the battle of Bosworth and was subsequently crowned King Henry VII. This brought the Wars of the Roses to a virtual conclusion and marked the beginning of the Tudor dynasty.

During the course of the Wars of the Roses, the Yorkist claim to the throne had passed to Edward Mortimer, Earl of March. By gaining the throne as Edward IV, a huge swathe of Marcher lordships had become Crown territory. The power of the Marcher barons was broken and the administration of the area was soon to be reorganised, with Welshmen playing a full part. This process was begun by Henry VII who set about rewarding those Welshman who had supported him in his fight for the Crown.

CHAPTER 3

Tudor Times

The 16th century was a time of rapid change, religious, economic and political. There were six successive sovereigns in power each attempting to impose their beliefs and prejudices onto their people—Henry VII, Henry VIII, Edward VI, the unfortunate Lady Jane Grey, Mary Tudor and finally, Elizabeth I.

By 1498, Edward, third duke of Buckingham, inherited his father's vast estates, Hay and its castle being but a small part of his inheritance. Almost immediately he set up a council to investigate, assess and implement payment of all dues owing to him. At the time of this survey not only the castle but the town itself was adjudged ruinous—little wonder, after all the battering it had received in the previous three hundred years. The duke's survey caused open insurrection amongst his disgruntled tenants at Brecon but it seems that the depleted population of Hay accepted the inquisition without protest, at least none has been recorded.

In 1505, under pressure from numerous petitions from his Welsh subjects, Henry VII issued a series of charters removing restrictions on Welshmen taking up positions of power and being allowed to purchase land and property. A posthumous victory, one might say, for Owain Glyndwr.

The existing legal system consisted of a series of courts. The court baron was an assembly of customary tenants under the presidency of the lord of the manor and the court leet was attended by freeholders and tenants; Welsh and English Hay each held their own courts.

The administration of the local manorial court was complicated and open to corruption for it came under the jurisdiction of the steward. It was held every few weeks, usually in the Town or Guild Hall. In Hay, juries were sworn in on the steps that led from the market square to the main gateway of the castle which was once a place of refuge for those wishing to escape arrest. The manorial court dealt with minor domestic disputes, obstructing the highway with dung hills—at one time the local doctor seems to have been the worst offender—and numerous cases of drunkenness and rowdy behaviour.

Great Sessions was a higher court held every three or five years in which more serious offences such as felony, rebellion, trespass and false imprisonment were adjudged and reviewed. Pardons could be granted at these hearings, unfair judgements reversed and fines re-assessed. It was, in effect, a court of tribunal.

Tenants were obliged to attend these courts but in some areas, Hay included, the lord of the manor collected bribes in collusion with corrupt officials in order to ensure the outcome of proceedings. This gave great encouragement to criminals and, not surprisingly, the law-abiding members of the community objected to 'the discharge of felons, rioters and other misrule people'.

In 1518 angry tenants of Hay joined those of Brecon to add their voice to a protest made at the Court of Star Chamber, the people becoming so angry the government had to intervene. Buckingham's officials, and ultimately the duke himself, were strongly reprimanded by the King for their part in the corruption. He was ordered to ensure that regular, properly administered courts were held and from 1521 it was decreed that Great Sessions would be held twice a year and for not more than eight days' duration. Furthermore, the practice of coercing tenants into redeeming sessions was made illegal and when the King went on to appoint itinerant justices to conduct these court sessions this did much to remedy the situation.

1521 was also the year in which Henry VIII had Edward, third duke of Buckingham, beheaded on suspicion of Treason. He seems to have been a man as obnoxious as his father had been and was so hated by the people under his control that on a visit to South Wales he required an army of bodyguards to protect him. At the time of his execution he was 43 years old and the holder of vast estates bringing in an estimated income, then, of £6,000 a year.

From 1527 onwards Henry VIII was preoccupied with trying to obtain papal dispensation to release him from his marriage to Catherine of Aragon. His long struggle with the Pope culminated in the rejection of papal supremacy and the Act of Supremacy of 1534 which asserted that Henry was to be the supreme head of the Church of England. Between 1535 and 1539

Henry, through his Vice-General, Thomas Cromwell, systematically destroyed monasteries throughout the country, including the priories at Llanthony and Brecon, commandeering much of their wealth by selling off vast quantities of ecclesiastic gold and silver plate as well as land to already wealthy landowners.

After the Dissolution of the Monasteries Henry VIII turned his attention to the state of the Anglican Church throughout the land. He ordered that clergy should be responsible for keeping a record of all births, deaths and marriages within the parish. The duties of the Hay Parish officials were similar to those of our present day Parish Councillors. They were accustomed to starting their meetings in the vestry of the church before adjourning to a public house to deliberate, apparently adopting a rota to avoid any charge of partiality. The group became known simply as the Vestry and their duties included the maintenance of roads and bridges, the allocation and dispersal of alms, arranging apprenticeships and any other matters of concern to the community.

A good description of Hay in the 16th century comes from the pen of the antiquary, John Leland, who, in 1538, described it in this engagingly idiosyncratic manner:

> The Hay standith hard upon Wy and ytt shewith the Token of a right strong Waulle having in Hit iii Gates and a Posterne. Ther is also a Castel the which sumtime hath bene right stately.
>
> Within the Toune is but one poor Paroche. In the suburbe hard by Wy is a Parouche Chirche meately fair. There is also in the Suburbe a Chapel wher on a Sunday I hard Messe. Not far from the Parouche chirch in the suburbe is a great rounde Hille of Yerth cast up by Mennes Hondes other for a Wynd Mille to stond apon, or rather for sum Fortes of Bataille.
>
> The Town of Hay yet hath a Market but the Toun within the Walles is wonderfully decaied ... the Ruine is adscribed to Oene Glindour ...
>
> Dulesse a prety River rising in the Montinnes about iii Myles from the Hay cummeth even through the Toun and strait into the Wy without the Est Gate of the Toun. In Feldes hard by a Ploughyng hath been founde oftimes numismata Romanorum, the wich ther comminly be caullid Jewis Mony. The Toune longgid to the Duke of Bockingham. It pertaineth now to the Lord Stafford his sonne.

By this time Henry had turned his attention to the administration of the law. Ever since the reign of Edward IV there had been an embryonic border adminstration based at Ludlow; under Henry its powers were now increased to be able to act as a court of law, exercising both criminal and civil jurisdiction. In 1534, Rowland Lee, the portly Bishop of Coventry and Lichfield was appointed Lord President of the Council in the Marches of Wales. His brief was simple—to reinforce law and order, to bring about a uniformity of its administration and to eradicate all malpractice, bribery and corruption. This was a formidable task but one he relished for he was a heartless, censorious man, single-minded and impervious to the pressure of rank or privilege. He punished offenders with consummate satisfaction, more so if they were gentlemen—during his tour of office he once boasted of hanging 'four of the best blood in the county of Shropshire'.

In his fanatical pursuit of duty he was quite willing to degrade and torture those he considered at fault. It is estimated that within the six years of his presidency as many as five thousand men were hanged. Such was his terrible reputation that a visit from Rowland Lee was one to be dreaded. These brutal methods did, however, help to consolidate the laws that governed both England and Wales. In 1536, the first Act of Union was passed and the two countries were, at last, governed as one, after so many years of conflict and oppression.

Shortly before he died in 1547 Henry gave custody of Hay Castle to one James Boyle who was also lord of the manor. Unfortunately, he was no better than his predecessors and on one occasion was fined for the unlawful collection of tolls. He also employed a particularly vicious bailiff, William Smythe, who often resorted to assaults on market vendors, some of which ended in a court appearance. One such assault, however, ended in the death of a peddler, Ewan ap David, who wrote in his will:

> I am note sicke by God's visitacon but by the villany and hurts received at the handes of William Smythe now baylyf of the Hai.

The castle remained in the hands of James Boyle until the turn of the century.

After the King's death many of the remaining church properties were sold off by his son, Edward VI, and many more fell into disrepair. During his brief reign, 1547-53, all Latin services were abolished and the use of the English Book of Common Prayer legally enforced, leaving the Welsh speakers more

St John's Chapel used as a hairdressers c.1920

than a little confused; it wasn't until 1588 that even a Welsh Bible was produced, by one William Morgan.

The Guild Chapel of St John the Baptist, in Lion Street, had been used as a chantry for saying masses for individual souls, the first service of the day being held at dawn for people to attend on their way to work. However, after the Act Against Chantries was introduced in 1547, it, like many others throughout the country, was sold off and given over to secular use or simply allowed to fall into ruin.

Throughout the subsequent five year reign of Queen Mary Tudor many more churches fell into disrepair. Her persecution of Protestants was as vicious as her father's had been against the Catholics, and some 300 'Marian Martyrs' were burned at the stake, including Thomas Cranmer, the Archbishop of Canterbury and author of the Common Book of Prayer. This method of death, especially reserved for heretics, blasphemers and witches, had been devised to allow victims sufficient time in which to repent as the flames rose to consume them. There were, undoubtedly, a number of Welsh martyrs during this time but in general the people of Wales seemed to have been less openly subversive in religious matters than those elsewhere. But there were a few exceptions. Jan Morris, in *The Matter of Wales*, records several remarkable characters who were prepared to die for their beliefs. Among these, she says, were 'a bishop, a fisherman and a gentleman of Haverfordwest' who 'during the brief return of Catholicism under Queen Mary' were all 'burnt at the stake for their obduracy'. Taking the opposing view in 1593 was John Penry, a nonconformist of Cefn Brith, in Powys, described as 'a poor young man born and bred in the mountains of Wales'. He was hanged for treason for calling all Anglican bishops 'soul murderers'. This extraordinary character left behind four daughters called Deliverance, Comfort, Safety and Sure Hope.

It was only after 1558, when Queen Elizabeth ascended the throne, that religious extremes were largely abandoned giving way to a more tolerant attitude and some freedom of worship. By this time, however, the morale of the clergy of all faiths was extremely low. Many of the churches were derelict, quite beyond repair, and those that were still fit for use had no clergy to attend them. One disheartened bishop exclaimed that 'horses graze and alas, pigs are fattened in the houses once dedicated to God.'

Many parishes had no priest at all with the result that one curate might cover several churches some distance apart and few regular services were held. When a priest did manage to make an appearance as often as not he had travelled many miles on horseback and would come 'thither galloping from another parish'.

The lack of religious instruction was apparently having a disastrous effect on the population of Wales, judging by a complaint made by the Lord President of the Council in the Marches in 1573. He maintained that, in his opinion, people were far too concerned with 'empty sport and carnal pleasures, playing with dice and cards, dancing and singing with the harp, playing football, tennis, mock-trials and hostages and many other sinful sports too numerous to mention'.

We cannot know what provoked this stern rebuke. It could be that his travels through Wales had brought him to the little town of Hay, just when the inhabitants were letting their hair down during the May Fair celebrations. But it is surprising and rather heart-warming to realise that people still managed to enjoy themselves, despite their constant struggle against oppression, poverty and disease.

CHAPTER 4

The Manor House at Hay Castle

Following the Act of Union of 1536 and the continuing demise of the restric-
tive feudal system there was a marked increase in the number of vagrants
wandering the country looking for work. In 1572, in effort to control the situation, Queen Elizabeth I introduced the Poor Law which stipulated that each
parish should be responsible for the care of its own poor—as opposed to being
reliant on the charity of the Church—and that parish relief could only be given
to the destitute born within the parish boundaries.

Throughout the Middle Ages there had been a great deal of poverty in Hay
and in the days prior to the building of the almshouses and the Workhouse the
destitute's only hope was a place in one of the parish's special lodging houses.
These were rented by the Vestry especially for the homeless where they would
at least receive basic board and lodging. Work was also provided for those
who were considered fit which enabled them to help pay for their keep.

Not all Hay's residents were poor, however. By the beginning of the
century the castle had passed to Mary, granddaughter of James Boyle and
through her to her husband, Howell Gwynn of Trecastle. Thereafter, the
Gwynn family occupied the castle throughout the 17th century and were
responsible for the building of the manor house, much of which remains today
despite two disastrous fires in the course of its history.

In 1610, after a civil action and a fine imposed by the Attorney General for
malpractice, Howell Gwynn was granted the lordship of the manor of Hay
with all the benefits that went with it. But Gwynn appears to have been a
tyrannical bully like many before him and he was very unpopular with the
people of Hay. One of his more vocal detractors, a highly officious litigant by

the name of Eustace Whitney, of Pontfaen, lodged an appeal to the court against one of Gwynn's officials, Thomas Gwatkin, the bailiff of Hay, accusing him of:

> Taking tolls at the market held in Hay without authority, letting the market hall for the said baliff's own profit, and robbery of the complainant's servant and other misconduct in office.

The weekly market continued in Hay throughout the 17th century: in addition there were the Hiring Fairs held twice yearly where men and women from the surrounding farms could present themselves as available for hire for the following six months or a year; these fairs were, in effect, used as labour exchanges. They were also quite often the scene of much ribald enjoyment, providing a chance to meet friends, make deals and rekindle old feuds within the farming community lest they lose some of their fire. By six in the morning the streets of Hay were crowded with people who had come from miles around, many on foot, from the hills of Clyro and Painscastle to the north or from the Herefordshire borders to the east, paying their tolls on the ferry and again as they passed through one of the three main gates into Hay.

Once inside the town there was much to amuse them—numerous sideshows and stalls creaking with every sort of produce, including rabbits, pheasants, vegetables, boots, pots and pans; with travelling groups of musicians adding to the noisy chatter of the excited crowds.

There was also a great deal of drinking. Hay was well-known for its inordinate number of ale-houses for a population estimated at no more than 455, many of them, no doubt, staying open until the early hours of the morning.

Local trade would have been brisk and everyone set out to enjoy themselves except, perhaps, the likes of the resident kill-joy, Eustace Whitney, obviously still scornful of Hay's choice of bailiff. His complaint to the court of Star Chamber ran as follows:

> ... and the said markets and fairs are continually disturbed by all manner of dissolute and disorderly persons and notorious fellows, drunkards, rogues and vagabonds and such like bith men and women abiding from market day to another and consuming what they may get, in all ryotous kind of living without any punishment or correction of the same but are rather thereunto encouraged at the great offence annoyance and

hindrance of your majesty's faithful subjects dwelling in or near the same town, to the manifest corruption of the inhabitants ... who of late are growing to be like disposition to the said disordered persons ... allowed and protected by one John Thomas Gwatkin who so usurped and assumed the name and title of Bailiff of the said town being a man altogether partial towards office, a notorious common drunkard and known to be of bad behaviour.

Strong sentiments indeed from the sanctimonious Mr Whitney but it would seem that Thomas Gwatkin *was* rather a shady character for he again rented out the town's market house where 'corn, grain and victuals and commodities' were sold, to one David Morris for a yearly rent of £5 15 shillings. The rascal had pocketed the money, a fair sum in those days, leaving the good people of Hay to sell their wares without the benefit of cover or any protection whatsoever from the bitter east wind that howled through the narrow streets in winter.

While all this corruption was taking place in the market square, up at the castle work was progressing at a cracking pace. And whilst the likes of Eustace Whitney challenged Thomas Gwatkin, the rest of the country was at war again, this time between the Parliamentarians and the Royalists. Whether many men at arms were recruited from Hay is unknown but in 1642 the King was at Shrewsbury enlisting men to join the march on London and in all probability some men from the area may have joined them as Royalist sympathisers.

In January, 1649, King Charles I was executed, at about the time that Howell Gwynn's son, Thomas, and his family had moved into the newly completed manor house. This was attached to the remains of the Norman castle, the two buildings still called, collectively, Hay Castle.

By now the puritanising of the people of Wales was well under way. Cromwell's enforcers made every effort to stamp out the old religion and to that end a commission was set up authorising the destruction of the old established system of worship and the organisation of the new. Within three years some 278 clergymen, considered to be too traditional, were ejected from their livings.

The vicar of Hay, Thomas Dennis, was ejected on account of his Royalist sympathies and the town remained without a replacement for ten years. Many of the displaced clergy turned to works of scholarship or became schoolmasters but nevertheless the purge caused great hardship and many raised their voices in protest.

The Manor House at Hay Castle in the 1930s

Another fervent Royalist, Alexander Griffith, vicar of Glasbury, was fiercely opposed to the new legislation and was ejected for his views. He fought particularly hard against one of the government's approvers called Vavasor Powell. Griffith and his followers—the majority of whom were Welsh-speakers—bitterly resented his interference in church affairs and spurned the itinerant English-speaking preachers who were sent to replace their own Welsh clergy and restore the strictly Anglican Church. So hostile was the reception given these unfortunate replacements that recruitment was, understandably, rather slow and many parishes, like Hay, remained without clergy for a number of years.

These heavy-handed attempts to dictate religious policy were less than successful, simply creating the sort of conflict that breeds dissent. The latter half of the 17th century, following the Restoration, was a period of rapid recruitment to a number of dissenting groups that were springing up all over the country.

By 1665, dissenters were already establishing themselves in Hay, often meeting in private houses, much as the persecuted Catholics had done before them. A group of early Ana-Baptists in Hay, including James Hughes and Thomas Parry and their wives, were regularly charged at the Brecon Quarter

The Salem Baptist Chapel,
Bell Bank, in 2000

Sessions with 'not attending church'. These two men were further charged with 'not baptising a child' and in 1668, James and William Hughes and Elizabeth and Martha Gursum were condemned for being confirmed Baptists. And again, in 1684, the recalcitrant James Hughes and his wife, together with John Prees and his wife, were indicted for 'nonconformity'.

There were several nonconformist chapels in Hay, the earliest being the Salem Baptist Chapel, in Bell Bank, close to the Bull Ring. Established some time in the 1650s it was the second oldest in Wales. Rebuilt in 1878, the original chapel had a school-room at one end, used as the Goff School, endowed by Edward Goff, a wealthy London coal-merchant. The old Goff School was closed about 1850 and the trustees contributed to the cost of building the new British School in Heol-y-dwr, which occupied the site of the present police station.

It was during these unsettled times that the afore-mentioned Royalist agitator of Glasbury, Alexander Griffith, turned his attention to the lack of education for the children of Hay. His concern was justified for there was no official school in the town. In 1656 this was remedied by transferring the school at Talgarth to Hay, which was deemed in greater need of enlighten-ment. Mr Rice Powell, the current schoolmaster, moved with the school and received a salary of £40 a year, still grudgingly paid by the people of Talgarth. But by 1658, Alexander Griffith had somehow managed to inveigle his way into the position of schoolmaster at Hay, appointed by the same authority that he had so vigorously opposed a few years before.

There was still a great deal of poverty throughout the 17th century and the poor were treated, by today's standards, with appalling insensitivity. In 1696, for instance, William III decreed that all paupers in England and Wales should wear identity tags marked with the letter P on their right shoulders. Those daring to show any degree of obstinacy or false pride in this would stand to lose their charitable handouts. Alternatively, they could be whipped and given three months' hard labour in the House of Correction. More compliant paupers would receive a weekly pittance and, if their circumstances were really desperate, they would be given a little food, rough bedding and some worn clothing, donated by the more fortunate residents of the town.

The poor represented a perennial problem for the town's administrators and providing for them was a constant strain on community resources. Any poor from other parishes who were found in Hay were quickly moved on. Sometimes the unfortunate man or woman would be escorted to the parish boundary by the constable and ordered to return to their place of origin where, at least, they would be guaranteed a small measure of sustenance.

Of course, the lord of the manor and his family, visiting dignitaries and the town's more prominent worthies, were seldom directly troubled by the problems of poverty and squalor, though charitable acts were considered to be part of the landed gentry's way of life.

In 1684, the first Duke of Beaufort, Lord President of the Council in the Marches of Wales and Lord Warden of the Marches, made a grand tour of the Principality recorded in *The Official Progress of His Grace the Duke of Beaufort through Wales 1684*. The artist, Thomas Dinely, accompanied him, making sketches of the places they visited but these were so romanticised that they give no indication of the smell, dirt and disease that was an intrinsic part of the otherwise idyllic rural scenes.

In a sketch of the Guild Chapel of St John the Baptist, for example, which was then in use as a schoolhouse, the building looks fairly substantial but within a few years it was said to be in ruins and the falling stones and rubble were causing an obstruction in the pig market. In the same drawing several houses in Lion Street can be seen; as well as a Market Cross in the Bull Ring where itinerant preachers would either inspire or incite the bartering farmers and their wives with the fire of their oratory—or did they just ignore them, those chattering ladies of Hay, far too concerned with the rigours of their daily drudgery to pay them much mind?

Dinely also did a stylised drawing of the castle showing the newly built manor house and the two original gates in the castle wall. The first was at the bottom of the flight of steps leading to the Norman gateway and the second

Dinely's drawing of the Chapel of St John, then used as a schoolhouse

forming an entrance to the front terraces in Castle Street. The artist also included a number of domestic dwellings which appear, as it were, to be crouching humbly at the foot of the castle.

Fortunately, at some stage, Dinely put aside his paintbox to describe his visit to Hay:

> Teusday [sic] Aug 5 at noon having crossed the river Wye at Whitney ford or ferry in his chariot, his Grace was received by the High Sheriff, Gentleman and county troop of Brecon who first conducted him to Haye a market and castle town in Brecknockshire where his Grace and company dine a very handsome entertainment having been provided ... at the castle at Hay.

It really was a case of the rich man in his castle, the poor man at his gate. But there was one man who was extremely wealthy and yet concerned with

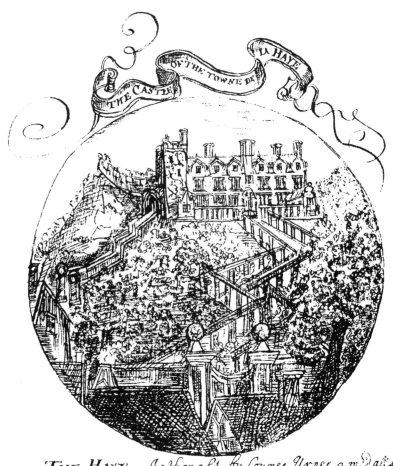

THE HAYE As thought by Coynes Urnes p m^ds there
found to have been an ancient Plantaton of the Romans and
since by later Ruines it appears to tco place of this History
sayth it may once sacked by Owen Glendour
& the vulgar Welsh callst his Town Y Gelhy

Dinely's drawing of the castle

the plight of the poor—William Pennoyre. According to the researches of
Geoffrey Fairs for his book, *Annals of a Parish*, William Pennoyre was a
wealthy Parliamentarian, born in 1606, the son of Robert Butler, a weaver and
glover at Dorstone 'who happened to be present when a man was killed ...
going to disguise himself he changed his name to Pennoyre'. In 1620, William
was apprenticed to a cloth-maker in London, learned his trade well and pros-

pered. Later in life his wealth enabled him to become a ship-owner with lucrative interests in the sugar industry in Barbados. In addition, his timely involvement in the manufacture of gunpowder during the Civil War enabled him to amass a considerable fortune. When he died in 1670 he left part of the revenue of his estates in Norfolk to:

> ... pay £12 for ever and after the death of my wife for the maintenance of a school in Hay in Brecknockshire where my desire is that children of the name Butler in the parish of Cusop and other poor children of the Hay whose parents cannot pay to be taught there, and forty shillings more for books for the said school.

The school, the exact position of which has not been established, was administered by the Almoners of Christ's Hospital, London. They seemed to have taken their responsibilities seriously and for many years regularly sent inspectors to oversee developments at the Pennoyre School. On one occasion, in 1691, they sent Samuel Crispe on a surprise visit to Hay. Unfortunately, he found the schoolmaster, William Watkin, with a diminished class of five or six boys. The inspector was not pleased and walked up to Cusop to the home of some of William Pennoyre's relatives, by the name of Butler. There he listened to one of the girls read and before leaving gave her and the other children twelve pennies each.

The next day he returned to the school and found that the luckless master had hastily scoured the streets and fields and managed to gather up a few more pupils: 'The best scholars rose and read out of the Bible', wrote Mr Samuel Crispe in his report. He seemed well pleased with the 14 girls and 35 boys present and found 'few of them non-readers'. Mr Crispe then 'admonished the children to come diligently to school and gave Mr Watkin 5s to divide amongst the children and they clapt their hands and their mothers blest me for coming to see them.'

The names of 20 of the poorest children were selected to receive grants from the charitable trust to allow them to continue their education, the four Butler girls being amongst that number. So, too, was 'the natural son of the Bayliff's son's begetting. Mr Hughes [possibly a governor] being somewhat against a Bastard being one. I said it was not the child's fault'. The poor mite was then listed amongst his class mates—the Thomas Lloyds, the Walter Proberts and the Mary Thomases of Hay—as simply, 'the Bailiff's boy'.

A National School was opened on the Brecon Road, Hay, in 1825, but it still accommodated children from the old Pennoyre School and charitable funding for the education of endowed pupils continued from the Pennoyre estate until 1923.

Thomas Gwynn and his wife had two children whilst they were living at the castle, a son, Howell, and a daughter, Elizabeth. The Gwynn family is commemorated in the choir vestry at St Mary's Church, on a stone that was originally in the chancel of the old church. It was Elizabeth Gwynn who founded an almshouse named after her. In her will she bequeathed a house to accommodate 'six of the most poor, weak and indigenous women of the town'. Whom should be chosen to occupy rooms in her almshouse was a decision that rested with 'the lord of the manor of Hay, the churchwardens and overseers of the town and parish and four of the most important inhabits and free-holders of the town'.

A further bequest ensured that

The Three Tuns stripped back to its timbers undergoing repairs in the 1970s

the revenue from rents of 58 acres of land in Radnorshire would be used towards the maintenance of the almshouse but through mismanagement or sheer negligence the original almshouse and adjoining property in Chain Alley, Newport Street, built in 1702, was deemed derelict by 1864. A local solicitor, James Spencer, who had been Clerk to the Trustees for some thirty years (he had also been Clerk to the Hay Tramroad) had earlier been charged with negligence in respect of the rents and, further to other irregularities in his book-keeping, he spent the last years of his life in Hereford Gaol.

After the death of Elizabeth Gwynn the family were obliged to rent apartments in the Castle to ease their financial situation. In 1702, one of the tenants was the extraordinary George Psalmanazar, a French-born imposter who claimed to have been born in Formosa and devised a unique Formosan

The Three Tuns (also known as Lucy's) in 2000

language. A friend of those in high places, including the Archbishop of Canterbury, Horace Walpole and Dr Johsnon, he was fluent in Latin and even wrote his autobiography in that language.

With the Gwynn almshouse having fallen into disrepair more homes for the destitute were needed. In 1832, six more almshouses were built, this time by Miss Frances Harley of Trebarried, in Church Street, with a further twelve houses on the Brecon Road four years later. These were funded by the income from two farms and were to be used 'as an asylum for poor but respectable women'—on condition they were members of the Church of England and resident in Hay.

In 1878, 'a row of six cheerful-looking houses each with its own grass plot and flower bed and fruit and vegetable garden at the back' named after Elizabeth Gwynn, was built in St Mary's Road to replace the original almshouse. Both sets of almshouses are still occupied today and are managed by voluntary committees, elected members and a clerk.

After the castle, the oldest buildings in Hay are the Three Tuns Inn, on the corner of Bridge Street and Broad Street, a cruck-truss, timber-framed building, and Brook House, in Brook Street, both of 16th century origin. There are also several fine 17th century buildings that still remain today— Tredegar House, The Pavement, close to the Clock Tower, formerly the King's Head Inn, is thought to be of 17th century origin. Nos. 2 and 4, Market Street, were also built at this time, becoming, in the 1900s, the premises of Hatters' Furriers, owned by R.H. Bondy, a rabbit-skin and wool merchant. It was here that the rabbit skins were cleaned, dried and graded before being shipped to Belgium, via Swansea, and from there exported to America to be made into hats. Undoubtedly, Pemberton House, in the Bull Ring, was formerly one of the finest 17th century buildings in the town. The front of the house was rebuilt in the 19th century and now that it has been converted into an hotel, The Kilvert Country Hotel, it has suffered still further modernisation. The Café Royal, in Broad Street, also dates from the 17th century as does the stonework of a property at the top of Bear Street, close to the Bull Ring, formerly the The Bear Hotel, with its exposed 16th century timbers above.

Finally, a fitting exit from the 17th century, taken from Jan Morris's, *The Matter of Wales*. She writes of an extremely puritanical squire called Colonel Jenkin Jones from Llandetty, in Usk, who, being also a practical man, had taken over his local church for use as a barn during the brief period of the Commonwealth. When he heard that Charles II had ascended the throne and intended to restore the Anglican establishment he apparently had a brainstorm and, mounting his horse, cried: 'Ah, thou old whore of Babylon, thou'lt have it all thy own way now!'

With that he fired his pistol at the vestry door—the bullet hole can still be seen—and galloped off down the Brecon Road, never to be seen in Llandetty again.

CHAPTER 5

Eighteenth Century Hay

By the end of the 18th century many goods that had been traditionally produced by groups of local craftsmen were now being mass-produced in the vast factories that were being especially built to accommodate the latest innovation, the steam-powered machinery. The Industrial Revolution was well under way, marking the end of the old cottage industries and the gradual transfer of labour from the land to the factory floor with the promise of higher wages. But in Hay the change took longer and the town's economy remained largely one of local produce meeting local need. For instance, those called for jury service in the 1770s were listed as craftsmen and artisans—saddlers, tailors, blacksmiths, mercers, flax-dressers, watch-makers, curriers, coopers and shoe-makers. The turning point came, however, almost a century later, when the railway reached Hay, opening up trade in goods that were mass-produced elsewhere, a development with which local craftsmen could not compete.

For so long this insular and self-sufficient economy had enabled the lord of the manor to control trade and ensure that it was monopolised by the rent-paying burgesses, thereby pocketing much of the profit. It was a time when the working life of poor men and woman was long and arduous, starting at a tender age. Children as young as seven were apprenticed to local people, ostensibly to learn a trade but in effect many ended up little more than general servants.

In Hay, it fell to the Vestry to organise the placement of apprentices but it was often felt that having an apprentice was more trouble than it was worth—so much so that at one stage the Vestry had to set up a lottery to determine which tradesmen would be obliged to take on a young person, the winners being the ones who drew blanks.

There were few concessions for children. In the rapidly developing industrial areas mill workers aged seven were expected to work from five o'clock in the morning until seven at night for a wage of one shilling a week. Youngsters from Hay employed on the land would have worked equally long hours. It is impossible to imagine today's seven year olds subjected to such a gruelling work-load in dangerous and unsanitary conditions and with barely enough to eat.

A maid in employment at Hay Castle, for instance, would have worked equally long hours for as little pay and, being the lowest member of the domestic staff, she would have been on duty up to eighteen hours a day. In addition she would be given all the most dirty and monotonous tasks in the household and only allowed an occasional day off to visit her family. Little wonder that life expectancy was no more than 50 and men and women looked old at 30.

Those inhabitants of Hay who were driven to crime through poverty and despair could expect short shrift from the law. Punishments meted out by the courts were severe. Some two hundred offences were punishable by death and a person could be sentenced to several years' transportation for a relatively minor misdemeanor. Court records of the period make harrowing reading. On 24 August, 1750, Thomas Prosser from Hay was charged with stealing two sheep belonging to William Gwyn Vaughan. He was found guilty and sentenced to death. Luckily, he was reprieved and transported instead. Three years later another resident of Hay, a yeoman called William Lewis, was charged with forging a letter: his sentence was 14 years' transportation.

A woman of Hay, Rachel Sparrow, stole nine silk handkerchiefs from John Price and was branded on the hand as punishment. Another woman, Sarah Magness, wife of a labourer, was sentenced to three months' solitary confinement for stealing handkerchiefs worth ten shillings. Yet, a few years previously, William Philips, a shoe-maker in Hay, was sentenced to only six months' hard labour for the manslaughter of Thomas Gilbert, having delivered a vicious blow to the stomach with his clenched fist, killing his victim instantly. The punishment for two women, Jane Thomas and Mary Barber, for stealing flour worth one shilling, was six months' hard labour.

It seems, therefore, that the meting out of justice was sometimes arbitrary and a fair sentence was merely a matter of luck. David Howell, convicted of a felony, received a sentence that was unbelievably harsh. He was to be '... whipped at the cart's tail, to receive 60 lashes, one minute to expire between each lash, to be confined with hard labour in the house of correction for 12 months and be whipped in like manner Saturday sennight before expiry of his sentence'. Three women also suffered the same fate.

In 1702, William Press, shoe-maker, convicted of petty larceny, was to be 'whipt at Brecon next Saturday and upon Thursday following at Hay'. In 1729, members of the court leet were petitioned for 'a whipping post, ducking stool, etc. to be provided by ye toun in a month on pain of 40s.'

Ann Edward, in 1736, was convicted of buying stolen goods and suffered the humiliation of being stripped 'at the conduit [one of the nine wells and watering places in Hay] the next Market Day and receive six lashes ...' Likewise Samuel Pritchard, convicted of stealing a ploughshare was given three months' hard labour and 'publicly whipped at the usual place' at the end of his sentence.

Offences against morality such as adultery, delay in baptising infants, defamation, holding heretical opinions and Sabbath Day breaking were heard in the Diocesan Consistory Court. Many of the cases were of excessively lewd or spiteful name-calling between feuding women but there were occasionally cases of clandestine marriage. This one was heard on 4 April, 1708:

I cite you Elizabeth Powell that you well knowing these things to be true [the reading of banns] did permit and suffer one Joseph Thomas to be clandestinely and privately married and joined in holy matrimony to one Anne Watkins at your dwelling house in the town of Hay.

1740 saw Richard Beavan branded a 'profaner of the Sabbath and also a common swearer and disturber of the peace'. Ten years later Richard Thomas was in court for 'suffering his son to drive a cart on the Lord's Day'.

A regular offender of public decency seems to have been a Dr Lyde who caused great offence with the putrid dunghill outside his house which he seemed reluctant to move. There was also a concerted effort by the people of Hay to effect the removal of John Baynham's pig market (in Pig Lane, now called Chancery Lane) which was causing offence.

Anyone caught 'forestalling' was punished, of course, as dealing on the roads into Hay before the bell was rung for the market to commence deprived the lord of the manor of his revenue from tolls on 'official' sales. Mary Higgins found herself in court, for instance, for 'buying fowl and eggs before time out of the market place'. She was fined 10 shillings and a year later Elizabeth Price and Rebecca Tompkins were charged with the same offence,

*Later 'players'—a Dancing Bear with its Italian handlers
photographed outside the Blue Boar in 1909*

as were Henry Lilwall and Joshua Thomas, caught red-handed by a sharp-eyed bailiff.

In fact, *bona fide* traders were taxed several times over. In additon to the tolls on the ferries or at the town turnpikes they had to pay rent for their stalls and a further toll on each of their sales—four pence on the sale of a bull, for example, six pence for a cow or calf, three pence for a billy goat and one penny on a bundle of vegetables.

In 1741 some strolling players were obliged to pay two pennies—more than a day's wages—for the ferry across the river as the ford was submerged. All these tolls, taxes and dues were collected by the market officials and added to the coffers of the lord of the manor. Attempting to avoid paying for the ferry by using the ford was risky and accidents were no doubt frequent.

But it was at the fairs that the poor enjoyed themselves as best they could and new clothes were the order of the day for even the lowliest of servants. As farm labour was hired at one fair and paid off before the next, fair time was usually the only occasion when there was money available for such extravagance. On the day of the fair the women would arrive in Hay in their worn and patched clothing, mud-splattered from the journey. On arrival they would buy something new at one of the outfitters in town, if they could afford it, a pretty bonnet or a pair of shoes and, at the end of the day they would change back into their old clothes for the journey home.

1740 was the year that saw the death of William Seward, a Methodist preacher who had come to Hay in search of converts. He was a determined evangelist and for some years previously he had been an active campaigner for Charity Schools for poor children. He met John Wesley in 1738 and the following year sailed to America hoping to establish an orphanage in Savannah and a school for oppressed black children in Pennsylvania. When the money ran out he returned to England to raise funds and for a while joined up with the fiery preacher, Howell Harris, on a tour of South Wales. However, many of the people he met took exception to his preaching and reacted violently. Seward was attacked on a number of occasions, once sustaining a vicious punch in the eye that nearly blinded him.

The old Wesleyan Chapel on the Brecon Road, built c.1769,
but demolished in the early 1950s

Some people believe that Seward was attacked and killed whilst preaching on Black Lion Green but in fact he died from injuries previously sustained during his journey through Wales. His journal poignantly records the days leading up to his death:

> Came to Hay and attempted to discourse a little distance from the town but after singing and prayer and discoursing a few minutes the Minister of the parish and several justices of ye peace with many other clergymen came and demanded my silence and stirred up the people against us.

When Seward attempted to resume his preaching on Black Lion Green he was again faced with a hostile crowd. Fearing further attacks the vicar of Hay intervened and prevented him from preaching. Seward died soon afterwards and is buried under one of the ancient yew trees in St Mary's churchyard at Cusop. He will be remembered as a philanthropist of conviction and a man of great courage.

Despite the hostility met by William Seward, by 1769 a Wesleyan Methodist Society had been established in Hay and John Wesley himself made his first known visit to the town the following year. He preached several times at the chapel which stood at the junction of St Mary's and Brecon Road. Though the numbers of practising worshippers had dwindled the membership was maintained and in 1850, the Wesleyans moved to a larger chapel in Oxford Road, whilst another faction—sometimes referred to as 'primitives' on account of their liking for outdoor services—built their own Bethesda Chapel in 1865, later called the Elim Church and now the Bethesda Evangelical Church. There is also a small Apostolic Church in Newport Street.

The Quaker Society of Friends have also had a small following in Hay since the 17th century but as they, and other early nonconformists, were often hounded by local clergy and neighbourhood bigots, meetings were sometimes held secretly in private houses. Many, of course, had emigrated to America in the 17th century in search of religious freedom. In 1765 there were meeting houses in the Red Lion Inn, (now the premises of T.A. Pugh and John and June Jones' grocery store) in Lion Street, The Swan and the barn of The George Inn—though these were not secret but officially licensed as 'proper places for the people called Quakers to assemble and meet for Divine Service'. At a later date, 4 High Town, now Pemberton's Bookshop, was also used as a meeting house for dissenters.

From the middle of the 18th century many of the 'fire and brimstone' school were preaching through Wales and the revivalist movement was well under way. As Jan Morris observes in her book, *The Matter of Wales*:

> Their rhetoric was often majestic, their techniques were theatrical. Christmas Evans, the one-eyed Baptist virtuoso of Llandysul, in Dyfed, was said to make his congregation tremble just by his Cyclopian glare ...

In Gwent, the energetic Independent minister, Edmund Jones, who, in addition to writing a book on ghosts, travelled extensively on the back of a donkey, evangelising as he went, preached a total of 511 sermons in the year 1773. In his will he decreed that he wished to be buried in a separate grave from his wife as he 'didn't want there to be any difficulty on the day of resurrection'.

Such was the fire and magnetism of some of the great revivalist preachers that their congregation would sometimes feel moved to clap their hands for hours on end after a particularly rousing sermon whilst others would take to jumping up and down in a frenzy of jubilation.

Persecution of dissenters continued for many years. A hundred years later, on Sunday 21 May, 1871, that incomparable diarist, Rev Francis Kilvert, curate of Clyro, near Hay, wrote: 'After Church visited some of the cottages. Elizabeth Pugh told me that when she was living at Pen-y-fforest

The United Reform Church, now The Globe Gallery

41

she used to go to the Baptist and Independent Chapels at Paincastle. Stones were frequently thrown into the Chapels among the congregation during service, and once a dog was hurled in. There was a great laugh when the dog was seen flying in.'

And on Good Friday, 1872, he records that: 'An election of a Guardian for the parish is coming on and the place is all in an uproar of excitement. Church versus Chapel and party feeling very high. The dissenters are behaving badly.'

On a more practical note, a number of buildings in Hay are of 18th century origin though, of course, many have since been drastically altered—façades have been rendered, roofs retiled and houses converted into shops. Unfortunately, many of the original features have been destroyed in the process and replaced by unattractive additions, yet the resulting hotchpotch of styles, though architecturally bizarre, is not without a certain charm.

CHAPTER 6

The Victorian Age

In 1837, the young Queen Victoria began her monumental reign, one that would continue into the next century. As for Hay, by 1809, Henry Wellington had become lord of the manor. He also owned, and was later to occupy, the castle where petty criminals were still incarcerated pending appearance in court. Perhaps finding this arrangement inconvenient he instigated the conversion of St John's Chapel in Lion Street into a lock-up with two cells and accommodation for the gaoler above. The barred window of one of the cells can still be seen from inside the building.

The inordinate number of ale-houses in Hay for an estimated population that had now risen to just under 1,000 had always been a contributory factor to the rowdy and wanton behaviour in the town, especially during market days and fairs. To combat this, by the mid-1850s the small band of law enforcers in Hay had grown to five—a Superintendent of Police and four constables. These gentlemen, however, were not the pillars of society one might imagine. The Superintendent, William McMahon, and two of his constables were themselves in the court of Quarter Sessions charged with assault and wrongful arrest—reminiscent of the bullying bailiff, Thomas Gwatkin. In this instance they were acquitted but McMahon was later found guilty of a similar offence, sentenced to a month's imprisonment and fined £5.

It was just as well that the Superintendent of Police was spared the ignominy of being locked up in his own gaol for he was clearly a very unpopular man. When he returned to Hay he was surrounded by a hostile mob armed with stones, and had to seek refuge in the postman's house. However, the jeering crowd would not disperse and the vicar hurried from the castle in an attempt to intervene and pacify the crowd. Evidently they decided to turn on him instead and in the course of the altercation he was struck by one of the stones. McMahon eventually managed to escape and left Hay the following day only to appear at Brecon Assizes later that year on a charge of perjury brought by the landlord of The Black Lion Inn. On this occasion he was found guilty and transported for seven years. So much for law and order in Victorian Hay.

Not that certain members of the Church were any better, setting a bad example for their flock. In his entry for Wednesday, 7 February, 1872, Francis Kilvert described Parson Williams of Llanbedr as 'a good churchman but he was a very drunken man ... He was very quarrelsome, a fighting man, and frequently fought at Clyro on his way home from Hay. One night he got fighting at Clyro and was badly beaten and mauled. The next Sunday he came to Llandbedr Church bruised black and blue, with his head broken and swollen nose and two black eyes. .. My brethren,' he used to tell his congregation, 'don't you do as I do, but you do as I say.' He read the sermons 'very loud and he was a capital preacher'.

Life for working people everywhere, and especially in rural areas, was still one of unremitting hardship. Very little had changed since the previous century and those who resorted to stealing food or goods, often of little value, were still dealt with severely. So, too, were those who, despite the punitive laws, still took to the road—pedlars, tinkers, fortune tellers, jugglers and wandering groups of play-actors. During the reign of George III much common land had been enclosed to make smaller, more manageable fields, bordered by hedges. This meant that smallholders were no longer able to graze their few animals and thereby make at least a subsistence living. The result was that more and more people took to the road in search of casual work. In 1824, in an attempt to control the situation, a new Vagrancy Act identified three main classes of miscreant punishable by law—'idle and disorderly persons', 'rogues and vagabonds' and 'incorrigible rogues'. In 1864, hard labour as a punishment was introduced as an alternative to transportation which was expensive and difficult to supervise. If a man or woman, or even a child, was sentenced to hard labour it meant just that. It entailed a terribly harsh regime that included a variety of mindless tasks—the turning of a crank, under a 12lb pressure, up to 10,000 times a day; or walking the treadwheel to a height equivalent to Ben Nevis, sometimes pumping water to supply the prison system. These punishments were both cruel and pointless yet both treadwheels and cranks were still being used, even for children, until 1898, when an Act of Parliament banned their use in Her Majesty's prisons. In Gloucester Prison the stocks were still being used until the second half of the 19th century. There had been stocks in Hay, of course, since the Middle Ages, where miscreants and ne'er-do-wells would be put on public display on market days, exposed in their shame and subject to all the jeers and jibes and flying missiles their enemies could muster.

Somehow less barbaric than the treadwheel or the crank but still a hated form of punishment was 'picking oakum', which was considered to be particularly suitable for women and children. The work involved untwisting and teasing out lengths of old, tarred marine rope which, in the cold, damp atmosphere of the cells made the flesh of the fingers raw and excruciatingly painful.

The Chapel of St John had, by then, been put to secular use and the premises were subsequently used by a baker, a butcher, a saddler and a hairdresser and at one time, as a schoolroom. Part of the chapel is now used as a place of worship once more and various rooms are available for public meetings and other community functions.

Whether the fact that for most of the previous century there had been no vicar in Hay had any bearing on the endemic intemperance is uncertain, but the parish church of St Mary had been so often left in the care of curates or

St Mary's, taken from South Wales Illustrated in a set of Pictures *by Henry Gastineau, c.1830*

churchwardens that both the morale of the church members and the fabric of the building itself were in a very bad state.

In 1828 the old church was described as 'dark, comfortless and ill-contrived and quite inadequate in point of size'. Most of the pews were reserved for the town's more prominent residents leaving little room for anyone else. However, in 1831, Hay had its first stipendary curate, Rev Humphrey Allen, who decided to resolve the problem by raising enough money to rebuild the nave in 1833, one which was more spacious and fairly comfortable. Even so it is generally agreed that the original 12th century church was architecturally far superior, but all that now remains is the lower part of the tower and the south doorway.

He also provided a piece of land close to the Dulas Brook for the first gas works in Hay in 1840, a private enterprise instigated by local tradesmen, and the gas street lamps were installed a year later. Electricity came to Hay much later, in 1929, although there was an earlier, private supply in Brook House in 1913, the dynamos powered by two gas engines.

Rev Humphrey Allen's successor was Rev William Latham Bevan, made famous through his friendship with Francis Kilvert. The latter was a frequent guest of Bevan and his family at Hay Castle where he would join them on the lawn for tea, a jolly game of croquet and a spot of archery in the field opposite. How could he resist these invitations, guaranteed the company of the vicar's charming daughters and their pretty young friends, in particular young Daisy Thomas, to set his heart a-racing?

William Bevan came to Hay as a young man of 25 in 1845, resided at the Castle, which was then owned by Joseph Bailey, lord of the manor, to whom he was related by marriage, and remained for 57 years. Though austere, autocratic and steeped in strict Victorian values he was a tremendous asset to the community. He organised the building of the chancel and apse to the church in 1867 and was the author of the *History of the Diocese of St David's*. He also worked tirelessly to raise the standard of education at the National School on the Brecon Road which was largely funded by voluntary contributions, including a sizeable sum from his predecessor. The school was maintained by further donations and an annual grant of £14 from the trustees of the old Pennoyre School, which had formerly done so much to help educate poor children in the parish, some of whom were resident in The Union Poor Law Institution or Workhouse, sometimes referred to as 'The Spike'.

The Spike (later called Cockcroft House, then renamed Frank Lewis House and now Union Mews) was built following the 1834 Poor Law

Amendment Act, whereby each parish was obliged to provide accommodation for its 'law-abiding paupers'—widows, children and the disabled—as opposed to wandering 'rogues and vagabonds'. This Poor Law Institution was erected near the church in 1837, and run by a locally elected 'Board of Guardians of the Poor' through a governor and a matron in charge with, officially at least, a surgeon and chaplain on call. But the conditions were spartan, the food basic and the rules strict—anyone failing to reach the gates by 6 o'clock in the evening, for instance, would be locked out for the night. Ending up in the Workhouse was a fate most Victorians feared.

There was, undoubtedly, a stigma attached to the residents, one which Rev Bevan, in 1849, tried to remove by admitting pauper children to the National School which was next to the Workhouse. It must be remembered that it was not until 1 September, 1891, that primary education was free—previously, children whose parents were unable to pay the fees were excluded. To emphasise his point he installed a gateway in the grounds of the Workhouse leading directly into the playground of the school. He also endeavoured to make Christmas in the Workhouse as festive as possible as described in this extract from an article in *The Hereford Times* of 1886:

> The men, women and children marched into the dining room in succession and took their usual seats in an orderly and becoming manner and at the signal all rose and together chanted a short grace. The Rev W Bevan, Chaplain, B.H. Allen, Esq. and J.E. Smith presided at the carrying of two halves of a splendid round of beef, nicely cooked and in good condition. Mr and Mrs Penrose, the master and matron, the head cook and Mr E. Powell, relieving officer, assisted in attending to the wants of the happy inmates. Each was given a heaped plateful of roast beef and baked potatoes and wonderful to relate, those who asked for more, unlike poor Oliver Twist, were immediately supplied with a second helping.'.
>
> Mr Smith addressed a few appropriate words to the paupers, telling them to be thankful to God for having put it into the hearts of the ratepayers to give them such a nice treat on this occasion ...

Their gratitude, it was suggested, might be shown by 'the old being contented with their lot and the young resolving to work hard so that they might one day be able to support themselves and do good to others.'

At six o'clock there was 'a plentiful supply of tea and cake' with the room 'lighted up on all sides by candles and Christmas lanthorns'. In the middle of the room was 'an elegant holly tree, covered with its vermilion berries and laden with toys for the children'. Whilst the children sat on the floor, the adults sat around the edge of the room 'in decorous and orderly array, looking pleased and contented'.

William Bevan was largely successful in raising the standard of education for the poor children of Hay but the degree of heavy drinking amongst the adult population, another of his concerns, remained, despite his sermonising and repeated remonstrations. In 1901, after a lifetime of service, William Bevan finally left Hay, just as the Victorian age came to an end, and died in Brecon in 1908.

Part of Francis Kilvert's duties as curate of Clyro was to visit and offer comfort to the poor in his own village and also in Hay, some of whom were living in Chain Alley. He writes with compassion of the deprivation he witnessed but on the lighter side these visits sometimes afforded him the sight of a pretty young girl which he would record with enthusiasm, as in this entry in March, 1870: 'In Chain Alley, Hay, at Prissy Prosser's door, saw

Chain Alley, Newport Street, c.1850s

Marianne Price grown tall and slight, her dark large eyes as beautiful soft and pure as ever.'

Four years later, whilst visiting the poor at the Harley Almshouses in Hay, Kilvert was rewarded by the sight of yet another pretty girl to stir his heart:

> The daffodils were nodding in bright yellow clumps in the little garden plots before the almshouse doors. And there a great ecstasy of happiness fell upon me. It was evening when I met her and the sun was setting up the Brecon road. I was walking by the almshouses when there came down the steps a tall slight beautiful girl with a graceful figure and long flowing fair hair. Her lovely face was delicately pale, her features refined and aristocratic and her eyes a soft dark tender blue. She looked at me earnestly, longingly and lovingly, and dropped a pretty courtesy. Florence, Florence Hill, sweet Florence Hill...

The Victorian era saw a tremendous surge in building throughout the country, both civic and domestic. In Hay a number of the earlier buildings were renovated and new ones built, some still in use today. In 1833, a prominent Quaker, William Enoch, built the Buttermarket in Market Street. It is a large, open-sided, stone structure, supported by pillars and still in regular use on market days and as a venue for numerous exhibitions, charitable sales and bazaars throughout the year. During World War II the building was commandeered by the Egg Marketing Board, the sides were blocked in with concrete slabs and the interior used as a store-room for emergency supplies. In 1983, generously funded by The Warren Club, a group of charitable local businessmen, the Buttermarket was re-opened and extensively repaired by Capps & Capps, a firm that specialises in the repair of old buildings and who had been working on Hay Castle after it had suffered extensive damage in a fire in 1977, more of which in Chapter 9.

In 1840, the original Guild or Town Hall, which may have been half-timbered, consisting of five rooms and an open space below, was rebuilt by the then lord of the manor, Sir Joseph Bailey. The new Hall incoporated an upper room sufficiently large to be used for public meetings and, at times, as a schoolroom or a place of worship. The space below was used as a Cheese Market. The riverside path, Bailey's Walk, was named after him.

To replace the dangerous ferries the first Hay bridge over the River Wye was built in 1763 with five stone arches, the builders being given a 98 year

A watercolour of Hay showing the replacement wooden piers of the bridge and the small landing stage near the water-mill where barges off-loaded

lease to collect tolls. But, after floods in the winter of 1795, three of the stone arches nearest to Hay were swept down river. Five wooden piers were then connected to the two remaining stone arches at the Radnorshire bank of the river. In 1838 *The Hereford Times* described this bridge as 'in a delapidated state with donkeys lying about causing alarm to the horses pulling the coaches ... Mr Baskerville's coach was almost overturned into the river when his horses took fright at the donkeys' and on another occcasion as 'a crazy old structure, spliced, propped and pitched in all directions, with dangerous approaches on each side with a short steep pitch with a tramroad crossing at the bottom and on the other side of the tramroad, the bridge gate.' No wonder that in 1825, according to the inscription on his tombstone, a local surgeon apothecary, John Charles Taylor, whilst out riding, decided to cross the river by the ford instead and in doing so, drowned. Not surprisingly, in 1855 the wooden piers incorporating the Hay side of the bridge were badly damaged by floods, parts being swept away down river, and again it had to be repaired.

In October 1861, perhaps belatedly spurred on by the earlier Rebecca Riots in Wales—in 1843 gangs of protesters had destroyed many turnpikes and to avoid identification had blacked their faces and worn female

The replacement bridge completed in 1864

clothing—300 people from Hay gathered on Hay Bridge having been led, erroneously, to believe that the tolls had at last been lifted. There was a great deal of cheering and shouting until they were told they'd been misinformed. A pitched battle ensued during which the bridge gates were torn down and thrown into the river. A full-blown riot erupted and the angry crowd, brandishing pick-axes and iron bars, wrenched off the spiked toll gate and smashed the toll house to pieces.

By the time the lease on the bridge expired at the end of 1861 the building of the new Hereford-Hay-Brecon steam railway was well underway. A new bridge was agreed upon which was built at a higher level to allow sufficient clearance for the workings of the new railway as it passed underneath along the line of the old horse-drawn tramroad. This had been used to transport coal from the mines of South Wales via the Brecon canal since 1816. The freight charge was 3d per ton/mile and the wagons carried passengers who could travel at the rate of 1d a mile. One pair of horses worked the western half of the tramroad and another the eastern section with the changeover set at Glasbury. The Hay to Eardisley section was added in 1818 which, two years later, was connected to the Kington railway. A painting of the Hay tramroad and a cast-iron wheel from one of the trucks are on display in Brecon Museum.

Crowds in Bridge Street celebrating the ending of tolls in 1933

The raised replacement bridge was completed in 1864. Six years later, Francis Kilvert, on one of his frequent walks into Hay described passing 'a chimney sweep with a cart and a pretty young donkey which shied at the train steaming under the bridge.'

The tolls were finally lifted on 30 March,1933, when crowds gathered on the bridge to genuinely celebrate. The present bridge, the third, was built in 1957.

The highway toll system as put in place under the local Turnpike Acts was complicated and open to abuse for there were a number of exemptions—foot passengers, agricultural vehicles, church-goers, people attending funerals or elections, post horses, wagons carrying soldiers' luggage or prisoners, horses going to be shod and the local vicar visiting the sick. Tolls were demanded and grudgingly paid on horse-drawn wagons carrying goods—like those belonging to Hay Carriers in the 1850s, that regularly travelled as far as Crickhowell and Abergavenny. There were no tolls, however, on dog-carts so many travellers used them for the conveyance of luggage and light goods on short journeys until they became illegal in 1854. According to Geoffrey Fairs in his book, *Annals of a Parish*, 'over forty of them were observed at the Hay May Fair in 1846, where the dogs were said to be exhausted'.

Francis Kilvert mentions dog-carts several times in his diary, having used one to take him to Hay Railway Station to catch an early train in May 1871. By this time, however, though still referred to as 'dog-carts', they were horse-drawn—in the spring of 1873 he used one to take him to dine at Whitney Rectory at which time it was drawn by an old chestnut horse called Rocket. Not all convenyances were ramshackle, however. The rich could afford to travel in style. Later that year Kilvert travelled 'in great state from Newbridge to Hay in a magnificent saloon carriage, in which Lady Baily [sic] had come down from London yesterday and which was on its way home'.

Far less grand was The Hay Omnibus, a horse-drawn contraption, which was used to meet the trains at Hay Railway Station to transport passengers up the steep rise into the town. This contraption was described by Kilvert on 13 May, 1871: 'Mrs Dew got out at Hay and went up to the castle in the only conveyance that Hay boasts now, a ramshackle filthy omnibus drawn by two carthorses, and driven by a man in a white slop with another agricultural labourer sitting by him on the box to open the door'.

After the castle, the most familiar landmark in Hay is the Clock Tower, identical in design to the one in Knighton, which was erected in 1866, at a cost of £600.

Another distinctive building of the time was the Agricultural Hall, in Lion Street, now one of Richard Booth's second-hand book shops. It was built in 1886 as premises for Robert Williams, manufacturers of farm machinery and tools, employing some 200 persons, including a number of apprentices. This business was the first in the town to become a limited company and such was the novelty of this that it became known locally as 'The Limited', a name Richard Booth retained when he bought the building. It is an imposing structure on two floors with an extensive basement, an ornate tiled frontage and a vast wooden ceiling supported by timber pillars.

Charming though the buildings may have been the Victorian age was still plagued by poverty and disease. The Local Board of Guardians, which had taken over the duties of the Vestry in 1836, tried very hard to improve conditions in the 302 dwellings in the town, housing, according to the 1861 census, some 1,997 persons. Some were apparently in a disgusting state encouraging the spread of all manner of diseases—including smallpox, cholera, diphtheria, scarlet fever and that scourge of so many Victorians, consumption. A case was recorded by Francis Kilvert in June, 1872: 'Mrs Prosser of The Swan [in Clyro], a young pretty woman dying I fear of consumption which she caught from her sister, Mrs Hope of The Rose & Crown in Hay'.

Such was the squalor in some of the dwellings in Hay that, in 1840, the Local Board viewed with some concern the case of George Wood, a shoemaker, who was summoned for keeping swine that were not in a 'wholesome and cleanly state' in his house. And the house of rag and bone man, William Arter, in High Town, was in such a mess it was deemed unfit for human habitation.

Prior to 1863, when the first Hay waterworks were instigated on Hay Common, these unhygenic conditions were largely due to the lack of an adequate clean water supply. In addition, as there was no sewage or refuse disposal the streets were filthy. As a result disease spread rapidly, often closing the schools for long periods. Scarlet fever was often the cause but in 1893 there was a case of smallpox in Turk's Common Lodging House in Chancery Lane. Three or four tramps who had been lodging there had to be isolated in a room at the Workhouse. Records show that, even though Dr Edward Jenner had developed vaccination against smallpox in 1796, there were still some isolated cases of the disease amongst the tramps there as late as 1902.

By now the Industrial Revolution was well under way but the drift from rural areas to the factories in the Black Country and elsewhere was not as strong in the Hay area as in other parts of the country. In many respects Hay continued much as before in that it was still a flourishing market, drawing

The Rose and Crown in Broad Street, sometime before 1890

traders from miles around. Corn had been sold in Hay since the early 17th century and there was a thriving trade in wool—the main sheep market being held in the last Thursday in June each year.

In 1848, the first Hay Show was introduced by the Hay and Wyeside Agricultural Society to promote the best in local breeding stock. It proved successful from the start and drew great crowds. A reporter on *The Hereford Times* felt moved to describe it in glowing terms:'Never has a more magnificent display of pure Hereford [cattle] been witnessed in a showyard in the Kingdom.'

In addition, before the present cattle market was built, the monthly street livestock sales were occasions of great importance in Hay. The cattle were driven into the town from the surrounding hill farms very early in the morning and sold from pens along the side of the road in Broad Street. Sheep were also brought in from the mountain slopes and penned on the pavement, behind the cattle. Pigs were always sold in Pig Lane, now called Chancery Lane. There was also a stray animal pound near St John's Chapel and another on the Brecon Road. One can imagine the chaos that ensued when a pig or sheep broke loose, or was let loose by local lads, charging through the milling

The open air china market in the Bull Ring c.1900

TheOld Black Lion Inn in 2000

crowds, crashing into stalls and causing the girls to squeal and cheer as the young men gave chase.

The markets were always well-attended and the revenue from them substantial. Besides a brisk trade in basic food requirements all manner of goods were produced in the town. Handmade nails, buckets and tools were sold from Robert Williams's emporium in Lion Street, so named when it had The Old Black Lion inn at the western end and The Red Lion pub where John and June Jones now have their grocery store. Agricultural implements could be repaired at a forge at the top end of Heol-y-dwr and there were a number of saddlers' shops selling all manner of harnesses and leather goods, and in the 1900s, the premises of H.V. Webb, Carriage Builder & Undertaker, (now Phil Gittins's Garage), could be found in Lion Street.

There was also an Ice House in Brook Street where ice was originally brought up from the river, mixed with salt and sold as a preservative in summer. During Victorian times, however, ice was brought weekly by horse and cart from Kington and stored in the Ice House.

There was a Salt House in Oxford Road and a total of eight malt-houses—one being in West House, Broad Street—although most of the ale-houses manufactured their own malt. There was also a cider works in Belmont Road and Tom and Fred Stokoe ran a soft drinks bottling works in the market square where the Midland Bank now stands.

Two interesting shops from the Victorian age remain in business today. By 1877, F.W. Golesworthy & Sons, Gentlemen's Outfitters, were already established in Broad Street, opposite the Clock Tower. Some members of the family still work in the shop, whilst others own The Granary next door—originally the premises of Charlie Jones, Wool Merchant—and The Blue Boar at the corner of Oxford Road. The distinctive Golesworthy signature was set in brass in the pavement outside the shop in the 1920s.

In 1884, Mayall's clock and watch-maker's shop opened in High Town, in which the late Mr W.E. Mayall, the founder's son, started as an apprentice in 1928 and worked until his death in 1998. In the photograph on page 109 April Ashley can be seen posing in front of the shop, the façade of which has changed little over the years. The business remains in the Mayall family and continues as a jeweller, clock and watch-mender to this day.

Victorian shop assistants worked extremely long hours as most of the shops stayed open well into the evening. *The Hereford Times* of 2 November, 1844, offered this unbelievably sanctimonious advice:

> ... the tradespeople of Hay one and all have come to the resolution of closing their shops at eight o'clock excepting Fair and market days and we hope that the assistants will appreciate this kindness by spending the time with a view to their physical, moral and intellectual improvement.

To this end they might choose to attend lectures or concerts at the Drill Hall. On Tuesday, 5 December, 1871, for example, they were offered the opportunity to listen to a lecture given by George Venables, the vicar of Clyro's brother, at Hay School—the subject, the German Empire. There were also Penny Readings, which were very well attended, where the audience would be entertained with suitably uplifting texts and recitations. Either that, or submit to one of Rev Bevan's thought-provoking sermons on the demon drink. To many of the inhabitants of Hay, however, the local pubs seemed a far better option and they continued to get drunk with some frequency.

One of the most interesting streets in Hay is Heol-y-dwr (pronounced Holy Door) , which, in living memory, had a stream running the length of it—disappearing under culverts to give access to houses and then reappearing—finally filling the millpond at the bottom of the hill where Peter Underhill's Garage now stands. The pond was in the forecourt and it was deep enough for children to float small dinghies on it. Water from the pond was channelled down the steep slope of Sheep pitch to the railway station where it was used for filling the huge tank that supplied the tenders on the steam engines.

Heol-y-dwr was once called Leather Bottle Street. (The Local Board took it upon themselves to rename the streets in 1871). As its old name implied leather bottles were once made there; No.1 Albert Terrace had been a tanyard, one of several in the street. There were also a couple of brickyards and at the bottom of the street near the river there were at least two watermills for grinding corn and a huge communal washing stone on which the ladies of Hay could take turns in thrashing the suds from their laundry.

During the reign of William III, all the dams and obstructions on the River Wye within Herefordshire (with the sole exception of the New Weir near Whitchurch where the owner had made a pound lock at his own expense) had been purchased by the county and destroyed thereby opening up the river for transporting goods. Close by the water mills at Hay there was the boatyard where at least two barges, both over 55ft in length, were built, the *Penelope* in 1807 and the *Liberty* in 1824.

Although the waters below Hay Bridge remained notoriously shallow and dangerous—a public notice in 1790 mentioned the dangers caused by 'floods, the coming down of large quantities of ice, and various other causes'— barges did come up from Gloucester, via Chepstow, bringing goods for Hay.

The corner of Bridge Street and Broad Street c.1900

High Town, c.1900

They were then loaded up with butter, cheese and other local produce stored in the cellar of a house in Bridge Street, known as The Stationmaster's House (where Mr Maurice John, Hay's last stationmaster, still lives) for the return journey. According to a report by a Mr W. Jessop of Bristol in August, 1805, approximately 11,250 tons of goods were exported from 'the Hay and Hereford to Bristol' and suggested that if navigation could be improved by increasing the depth of the water where it was most shallow the economic benefits to the area would be greatly increased.

Soap being an essential part of the woollen industry three soapworks were established in adjoining cottages in Bear Street and continued to operate until 1820.

At Christmas time there were the grand meat markets when local butchers took immense pride in displaying their wares, giving rise to much fairly good-natured rivalry. The live meat market was held in Broad Street, a fortnight before Christmas and started shortly after six o'clock in the morning. The street was lit by the gas-lamps, supplemented by the flickering oil lanterns carried by the traders, some of whom had travelled many miles to reach town.

Above: The earliest known photograph of Hay: Castle Street c.1870
Below: Castle Street c.1885; the building on the right was demolished in 1890

High Town c.1890 (Print taken from a magic lantern slide)

Broad Street looking towards the clock tower ...

Only the best quality meat was put on display and such was the reputation of the Christmas market that dealers from the Midlands and South Wales came to buy. The meat was laid out on gambos—low, flat carts—covered with white cloths. These were set out along the side of the road, surrounded by baskets, pens and boxes containing live poultry of every description—turkey, pheasant, hen and duck. Butter and eggs were also sold and when, two hours later, it was all gone, the traders would head for one of the six ale-houses in the street and settle down to some serious drinking.

The dead poultry market specialising in dressed birds was held a week later and started even earlier, at four o'clock in the morning. Eggs, cheese, fruit, holly and mistletoe were on sale and people who had managed to save a little money were soon caught up in the festive atmosphere and happy to splash out on their Christmas fare.

But the most fun was had by the children on the evening before the poultry sale. It was the custom for them to charge around the streets of Hay armed with sticks of chalk. If they managed to chalk a cross on the back of some unsuspecting adult they would call out 'Chalk night!' causing, no doubt, a great deal of annoyance and resulting in a few boxed ears.

The Hiring Fairs were still held twice yearly throughout the Victorian era, one in spring and one in autumn. Kilvert often mentioned them in his diary, making note of some of the more reprehensible behaviour he saw: 'Monday April 11 1870. Hay Fair and a large one. The roads thronged with men and drovers of red white-faced cattle hustling and pattering to the Fair, an unusual number of men returning drunk.' On Tuesday, 17 May, that year he wrote: 'Hay Fair today and tomorrow and I'm right glad to escape the noise, bustle, dust, drunkenness ...' A few months later, on Thursday, 15 September, 1870, he noted:'Hay Fair. Roads lively with men, horses and sheep'. Describing the drunken behaviour of people returning from the Michaelmas Fair in Hay on Monday, 10 October, 1870, he writes:

All the evening a crowd of excited people swarming about the Swan [in Clyro] door and steps, laughing, talking loud, swearing and quarrelling in the quiet moonlight. Here come a fresh drove of men from the fair, half tipsy, at the quarrellsome stage judging by the noise they make, all talking at once loud and fast and angry, humming and buzzing like a swarm of bees. Their blood is on fire. It is like a gunpowder magazine. There will be an

... and the other way towards Bridge Street, on market day, c.1900

Broad Street in the late 1800s

explosion in a minute. It only wants one word, a spark. Here it is. Someone has said something. A sudden blaze of passion, a retort, a word and a blow, a rush, a scuffle, a Babel of voices, a tumult, the furious voices of the combatants rising high and furious above the din.

Now the bystanders have come between them, are holding them back, soothing them, explaining that no insult was intended at first, and persuading them not to fight. Then a quick tramp of horse-hoofs and a farmer dashes past on his way home from the fair ... Tonight I think many are sore, angry and desperate about their misfortunes and prospects. Nothing has sold today but fat cattle. No one would look at poor ones, because no one had keep for them during the winter. Every one wants to sell poor cattle to pay their rent and to get so many mouths off their hay. No one wants to buy them. Where are the rents to come from?

And on yet another occasion, on Wednesday, 17 March, 1871, he wrote:

The great May Hiring Fairs at Hay, and squadrons of horse came charging and battalions of foot tramping along the dusty roads to town, more boys and fewer girls than usual. All day long the village [Clyro] has been very quiet, empty, most of the village folk being away at the fair. Now at 8 pm. the roads are thronged with people pouring home again, one party of three men riding one horse.

According to Geoffrey Fairs in *A History of the Hay*, Miss May Lilwall, once a nurse in the First World War, could remember in early youth seeing '... boys wishing to be hired standing on the day of the hiring fair in Broad Street, near where the farmers were with their animals, with a straw in the corner of their mouths as a sign that they are available for engagement.'

It is said that housemaids would advertise themselves by wearing their aprons, removing them once they had been successfully hired. Whereupon, no doubt, they would run off to enjoy themselves while they had the chance—perhaps to the Boxing Booth in the Bull Ring where local men would flex their muscles and try their luck with a few rounds in the ring with the champion, hoping to win 10 shillings and the admiration of the crowd. Or to the roundabouts, sitting astride the whirling 'Hills' horses, firmly clutching at the 'barley-sugar' poles—or maybe a ride on one of Studt's swinging gondolas. Even, maybe, partake of a piece of delicious toffee, called 'stick jaw', made by a Mrs Eve at 13, Lion Street, where she could be seen in the back kitchen, deftly stretching and pulling the long skeins of freshly-boiled toffee over a large nail before cutting them into lumps which she would then sell for ten a penny.

There was evidently a great deal of drinking at Hiring Fairs. Nor was Reverend Kilvert the only one to comment on the drunken behaviour he saw. The following memory comes from Florence Pugh, recorded in *A Pocket Full of Posies*, by Jen and Jon Conway:

> Streets were packed with showmen's paraphernalia round which crowds of townspeople and country folk would throng, always some indulging too freely in alcohol and becoming rowdy and unruly. There would be music, brightly coloured skittles and Aunt Sally booths, swing boats, roundabouts and dancing bears on collars and leads.

These pitiful creatures were still to be seen with their Italian handlers at fairs in Hay until about 1910. Dancing Bears (see photo p.38), often blinded and with their teeth and claws removed, were heartlessly teased and tormented by drunken crowds. When performing in Hay they were sometimes housed overnight in cellars beneath the Pavement, opposite The Limited, now Annie's second-hand clothing shop where the bars can still be seen. Francis Kilvert recorded the arrival of Wombwell's Menagerie, a travelling circus, in Hay on Tuesday, 7 May, 1872:

> ... the caravans which were looming in the distance along the Brecon road between the trees. The elephant a very small one, and three camels or dromedaries came shuffling and splashing along the muddy road in heavy rain looking cold and miserable and shivering as if they were wet through ...

The camels and 'wild beasts' were stabled at the Blue Boar, rubbed down with 'a wisp of straw' and were ready to perform by six o'clock.

> There was a fair lion and a decent wolf, which looked as if it had been just freshly caught, his coat was so thick and good and he was so strong and restless. A laughing hyena set us all laughing in chorus. A black sheep in the pangs of hunger was bleating piteously and had forced his body half through the bars of his cage to get at the biscuits the children were offering him. The exhibition was small and poor. A dwarf three feet nothing pointed out to us 'groups of wolves' stirred the beasts up with a long pole and made them roar ... The ground was in a swamp with pools of water and huge gaps in the canvas overhead let in the pouring rain.

Kilvert, however, with his compassion and love of animals, no doubt found the whole spectacle distasteful. Indeed, he ends his description with the words: 'I soon went away.'

It wasn't just animals who were often poorly housed. Housing for the working classes had been one of Prince Albert's special concerns, and rows of two-up, two-down terraced houses sprang up everywhere, often named Coronation Street and Jubilee Crescent in the poorer parts, or Royal Crescent, Prince Albert Mansions or Windsor Court for larger dwellings to accommodate the better off.

In the Hay area, Victoria Terrace was built in Cusop and Albert Terrace in Heol-y-dwr, building projects that would have met with unqualified royal approval. Her Majesty's displeasure can be imagined, however, had she known that on May 7, 1888, the Chief Constable's attention had been drawn to the Local Hay Board of the 'nuisance and annoyance at fairs by the use of water squirts and Ladies Teasers.'

A reporter from *The Hereford Times*, however, saw it all in much more romantic terms:

> Along the turnpike roads or paths through the fields might have been seen little batches of Welsh people bound for Hay, the men invariably with their coats slung loosely over their shoulders, the women arrayed in their gayest attire, with their delicate little hands encased in gloves, these being of every imaginable shade and tint under heaven according to the taste of the fair wearer. Pity them having to climb stiles with crinolines ...

A less wholesome vision was recorded by Francis Kilvert whilst walking into Hay in April, 1870: 'By the stile at the mouth of Boatside Lane I met old Sarah Williams travelling to market across the fields, regardless of stiles and walking with a large staff, a limb of a tree and looking like a bear with a ragged staff'.

The arrival of the new steam railway system in 1864 and the easy conveyance of goods from outside Hay had an adverse effect on the local craftsmen and tradespeople alike. Imported goods may have been inferior in many ways but they were cheaper and for people on wages far below those in the more prosperous areas of the country there was little choice.

As a result many local trades died out and businesses closed down. The blanket factory that took over the premises of Thomas Howell's flannel works in Castle Street (backing on to Belmont Road) had been forced to close, unable to compete with the steam-powered mills in the North and West Country. At the height of its productivity, in the early 1800s, the Howell flannel factory, using innovative machinery designed and made by Howell himself, had employed between 70 and 80 workers. By 1832, the Castle Street premises—which had been one of three mills owned by Thomas Howell—had become the property of H.R. Grant, printer, whose grandson, the late John Grant, newsagent and local historian, and his wife, Annie, occupied the premises until their recent deaths. The teasels used in the wool trade for raising the nap on cloth ready for trimming were cultivated locally and have since been the scourge of many a gardener in Hay.

Despite William Bevan's efforts to curb the drinking and riotous behaviour of some residents of Hay, the Guy Fawkes celebrations of 1869 were so rowdy that, according to an article in the *Kington Gazette,* some people were: 'in terror of their lives [as] burning pitch barrels were rolled down the streets, discharging rockets, crackers and squibs thrown into premises and even into cellars where stores of oil and combustible products were stored'.

Three policemen tried to intervene in this potentially explosive situation but had 'no control over the crowds of excited spectators'. They were bombarded with stones and one was wounded in the hand whilst 'a rocket scorched his whiskers'.

Such blatant anarchy would have met with the Queen's severest disapproval.

CHAPTER 7

Major Herbert Rowse Armstrong

When Queen Victoria died in 1901 the whole country was plunged into official mourning. Throughout her long reign, marked by so many far-reaching changes, she had remained a symbol of moral strength, duty and forbearance and many of her subjects felt a personal loss at her passing. As soon as her death was announced, in many homes the pictures were turned to the wall and curtains drawn. Older women in Hay would have reached for their best black, preserved in mothballs especially for funerals, and their hats would have been heavily veiled and swathed in black muslin. Although the more extreme late-Victorian styles may not have been adopted in Hay, fashionable young women were already taking advantage of the new paper dress-making patterns on sale in the Haberdashery store with material at half a crown (2 shillings, 6 pence) a yard.

An important feature in the town in the early 1900s was *Firefly*, the old fire-fighting conveyance, the steam from its boiler powering the water-pumps. At one stage *Firefly* was drawn by two fine black horses owned by the proprietor of the Crown Hotel who kept them in a field across the river. Though they were normally docile creatures, as soon as they saw the firemen arriving at the gate in their uniforms, ringing the bell and shouting 'Fire!' they would go berserk, galloping wildly around the field. It could sometimes take an hour to catch them but once between the shafts they would race to the scene at tremendous speed by which time, more often than not, the worst of the fire was over.

A subsequent team of horses remembered by fireman Percy Price were more co-operative. Once the gate to their field was opened and they heard the shout 'Fire!' they 'galloped across the field, rushed past him through the gate,

The Firefly *in Broad Street*

over the bridge, up Broad Street, past the clock, up Lion Street into the Bull Ring. There they would stand, stamping their hooves in eager anticipation, waiting to be harnessed to *Firefly*. They always ran on their own, day or night, getting more excited as they went'.

In the 1930s *Firefly* was replaced by a Fordson tractor and shortly before the Second World War a petrol-run engine was in action and the old *Firefly* was sold for scrap to aid the war effort. The present Fire Service, based on Brecon Road, has, of course, a modern appliance and ten fire-fighters on its duty lists, all of whom work on a part-time basis.

In 1901 the first telephone in Hay was installed in the new Telephone Exchange at the Post Office in Broad Street, now Dai Ratcliffe's Chip shop, with the number HAY 1. The Exchange later moved to separate premises on The Pavement.

Five years into the Edwardian age Hay was to see one of the most extraordinary episodes in its history. It was in 1906 that a diminutive young solicitor arrived in Hay, one who was to cause a sensation in the town and ensure for ever its prominence in the annals of crime. His name was Herbert Rowse

HAY PARISH
FIRE ENGINE.

NOTICE!

Is hereby given, that any person sending for, or using, the Hay Parish FIRE ENGINE, will be charged as under;

For any distance not exceeding One Mile - - 20s. per diem.
For every Mile in addition   -   -   *   - 5   ditto
For the person appointed to take charge of it - 5   ditto
For the Post Boy (if required)   -   -   - 5   ditto

And to pay for all repairs and damages incurred while out.

BY ORDER OF THE VESTRY.

October 1849.   W. HARRIS, PRINTER, HAY.

Armstrong and he was to achieve the dubious distinction of being the only British solicitor to be hanged in this country for murder. He was a small man, just five foot six and weighing a mere seven stones. Dapper in appearance, he was fond of wearing high, starched collars and a flower in his lapel and, in the fashion of the day, he wore his moustache long and meticulously waxed. He was a mild-mannered man, softly-spoken and extremely courteous, a stickler for form, the niceties of social intercourse and the maintaining of standards. Yet for all his pernickety ways he was popular in the town and commanded respect, having the upright carriage of a soldier. But perhaps his most striking features were his bright blue eyes which, though intent in their gaze, held the hint of a roguish twinkle.

Armstrong was born on 13 May, 1869, in Plymouth. His father, William Armstrong, was a colonial merchant and his mother, Eleanor, bore the maiden name of Rowse which her son was to retain throughout his life. Within his parents' social circle were Mr George Pearson Friend and his wife, Mary, a strictly religious couple from nearby Teignmouth. They had two daughters, Katharine, born in 1873 and Bessie, born two years later. Katharine was

71

highly strung but physically weak and susceptible to falls, accidents and every childhood complaint. In 1902, a bicycle accident left her blind in one eye, the effect of which lent a rather strained expression to her face. Shortly after the accident she had an attack of rheumatism in her left arm which reoccurred at intervals throughout her life and in 1904 she had a severe attack of influenza which left her prone to catching colds and neuralgia. She was so sensitive that the least nervous excitement brought on bouts of sickness and she became a martyr to indigestion.

For all this, young Herbert formed a strong affection for Katharine which was to survive their separation when his parents moved to Liverpool. Possessing a keen intelligence, he rejected his father's profession and chose to study law at St Catherine's College, Cambridge, his studies funded by the generosity of two maiden aunts. Their faith in him was rewarded for he worked hard, was a popular student and enjoyed university life. Gregarious by nature he made a number of firm friendships. One of these was with Charles Lisle Carr, who was to become Bishop of Hereford and a loyal supporter of Armstrong to the end of his life.

Armstrong's small stature made him a natural choice to cox his college's rowing team and in his final year, to his immense pride, he coxed the 'Goldie' crew, understudies to the Cambridge eight who were to challenge Oxford in the Boat Race that year.

In 1891, Armstrong graduated with a Bachelor of Arts degree and settled for a career in law. Four years later, at the age of 26, he was admitted as a solicitor with the Liverpool firm of Messrs Alsop, Stevens, Crooks and Co, and worked for them until 1901. It was during this period that he met Arthur Chevalier, another young solicitor, and they became life-long friends. He also developed an interest in the army and in May 1900, as a volunteer, he was appointed to the rank of Second Lieutenant in the 1st Lancashire Royal Engineers. In November of that year he was proud to be promoted to full Lieutenant and this military side to his life continued to be of tremendous importance to him.

In 1901 he decided to move to Teignmouth where Katharine and Bessie were still living with their parents. He became a partner in the firm of Hutchins and Co, remaining with them for two years until the partnership was dissolved, whereupon he took over the Newton Abbott branch where he prac-ticed on his own until 1906.

Whilst in Devon he continued his interest in the army. He joined the Ist Devon and Somerset Royal Engineers (Volunteers) and was promoted to

Captain. He also renewed his friendship with Katharine who, despite her inherent frailty and uncertain temperament, obviously attracted him with her intelligence and lively manner of talking. They also shared a love of music and although her frequent bouts of rheumatism hindered her, she had become a highly accomplished pianist. Even in her teens Katharine, plagued by chronic constitutional problems, developed an interest in homeopathy—she was regularly taking homeopathic pills prescribed for her and her life-long dependence on such remedies had already begun.

The relationship between Herbert and Katharine flourished and on 7 September, 1905, they became engaged. In June, 1906, Armstrong left Newton Abbott to join the firm of Edmund Hall Cheese, an ailing 63 year old solicitor with a solid practice in Broad Street, Hay. His premises, with the telephone number HAY 2, were directly opposite the offices of the only other solicitor in the town, Robert Griffiths.

At the time of Armstrong's appointment as Managing Clerk the two firms were able to co-exist quite amicably, finding sufficient custom to keep both practices busy. It seems that Mr and Mrs Cheese took an immediate liking to Armstrong—he even lodged with them for a while—and after a preliminary trial period of six months he was offered a partnership. With the introduction of £1,200 into the company he acquired a half share in the business. It was a proud day for Armstrong when the name of the firm was changed to Cheese & Armstrong and he felt that his prospects were sufficiently promising to enable him to marry Katharine after an engagement of nearly two years. The marriage took place at St James's Church, West Teignmouth, on 4 June, 1907. The bride was 34 years old and the groom 38. A photograph taken on their wedding day shows Katharine wearing a rather limp and shapeless frock, an image that suggests that sensuality or high fashion were not amongst her priorities: she is standing awkwardly, inclining slightly to the left where Armstrong stands erect, smiling and looking well-pleased.

After a short honeymoon in Switzerland the couple took up residence at Rothbury, a newly built house in Cusop, close to the beautiful and secluded area on the outskirts of Hay known as The Dingle. As the Hay office was little more than a mile away they had no need of a motor car. Besides which, both Armstrongs enjoyed walking, so much so that Katharine often accompanied her husband into town in the morning and then met him again on his return in the evening. The new bride took her duties very seriously and, furthermore, considering herself to be an astute businesswomen, showed an interest in her husband's work. Neighbours said later that they were a devoted couple and their relationship appeared to be amicable and affectionate, very much one of complementary equals. A year later, on 18 April, their first child, Eleanor, was born.

Armstrong continued to work extremely hard and the business in Hay prospered. He had always enjoyed playing a role in the life of the local community and was soon appointed churchwarden at St Mary's, Cusop. He also joined the Freemasons, enrolling at the Hay Loyal Lodge and, using his previous experience in the army, he set up D Company of the Brecknockshire Territorial Force in Hay. For recreation he enjoyed reading, listening to his wife playing the piano, gardening and the occasional game of lawn tennis.

On 20 February, 1912, when Katharine was nearly 40, the Armstrongs' second child was born—a boy, Pearson, who later acquired the nickname 'Sonny'—and by the end of that same year Armstrong and his expanding family moved to a much larger house closer to town. Mayfield was an impressive modern villa set back from the road behind a line of elegant cast-iron railings—it was one of the spacious late-Victorian houses to be built in the vicinity and no expense had been spared in its construction. There were a number of outbuildings including a stable for two horses above which was a coach-house to accommodate a groom. The house also had its own three acre paddock and substantial fruit and vegetable gardens. With its sweeping driveway, shrubbery, flower gardens and grandiose style Armstrong could feel that life was treating him well.

Though very much a family man—his wife and children were the mainstay of his life—though, as a typical Edwardian husband, he left the household management to his wife. Despite being apt to crumble under stress she nevertheless organised her three domestic staff efficiently—Emily Pearce who had started as a nanny and, still called Nana, stayed on as a housekeeper; a maid, Harriet Price, recently widowed; and Lily Candy, an undermaid, later to be replaced by Inez Rosser. The garden, however, was Armstrong's responsibility and it became something of a preoccupation. Although he was able to employ a gardener, William Jay, the maintenance of the extensive grounds at Mayfield became a perpetual headache. Surrounded by open fields it fell prey to weeds, in particular that perennial scourge of all gardeners, dandelions, especially on the paths in the vegetable garden and along the driveway and Armstrong and Jay spent a great deal of time and effort trying to eradicate them. He'd even got Miss Pearce and Harriet Price weeding on their hands and knees, a laborious task and not very effective when dealing with the more tenacious, tap-rooted plantains growing in the lawn.

Jay had previously managed to keep the situation under control by buying patent weed-killers but with a wife as frugal as Katharine Armstrong much preferred to make his own weedkiller as he considered patent preparations not only less effective but also far too expensive. Having found a likely recipe in a copy of *The Times* he had cut it out and kept it in his garden file in a small cupboard by the fireplace in the study.

On 2 May, 1914, he purchased a quarter pound of arsenic from John Frederick Davies, the chemist in High Town in Hay. When making the sale Davies asked Armstrong what he wanted arsenic for and was told the purpose. The chemist explained that, as required by law, he would have to tint the white arsenic with some colouring—either soot, charcoal or indigo, to prevent it being mistaken for any harmless white substance such as salt, flour or bicarbonate of soda. In this instance Davies tinted the arsenic with charcoal and asked Armstrong to sign the Sale of Poisons Book. It was a procedure he must have performed many times whilst serving other local gardeners with arsenic for precisely the same purpose.

Armstrong mixed the arsenic powder with that of caustic soda in equal proportions of four ounces each. He then made a concentrated solution by adding a gallon of water and boiling it on the kitchen range, using an empty petrol can. He then poured the concentrate into an old port wine bottle and from this bottle the solution was diluted for use—one gallon of water to one tea-cup of weedkiller. All the contents were used on the weeds that same afternoon and the empty bottle was put away in the loft above the stable and never brought back into the house. The surplus caustic soda was put back in a tin and kept in the study cupboard, along with all the other gardening paraphernalia, including a rose spray and insecticide solution normally used by Katharine, who took a particular interest in the roses.

Such was the pattern of life for Armstrong and his family, a fairly conventional existence in many ways, but comfortable. His involvement with the Masonic Loyal Hay Lodge and the Territorials, his appointment as Clerk to the Magistrates Court and his regular attendance at the parish church ensured a full professional and social life, one that guaranteed him the acquaintance of the most influential names in Edwardian Hay society. But in 1914, at the outbreak of world war, everything changed and events in Armstrong's life began to lead irrevocably towards disaster.

On 26 April, 1914, Armstrong's partner, 71 year old Edmund Cheese, died of cancer of the prostate and the following day his wife died of a heart attack. This gave Armstrong the opportunity to buy the remaining half of the business and the brass plate was again changed, this time to: Herbert Rowse Armstrong, Solicitor. No sooner had this been done than Britain declared war on Germany. Forced to leave Edmund Cheese's nephew, A.C. Sampson, in charge of the office, Armstrong was posted to the south of England to join a contingent of the Ist Wessex Field Company, Royal Engineers, with the rank of Captain. He was engaged for the most part in administrative duties where his meticulous eye for detail and rather pedantic attention to form was especially useful.

Herbert Rowse Armstrong

While Armstrong was away Katharine arranged the renting of Mayfield and went to live with her mother in Teignmouth so that Armstrong could visit her and the children when he was on leave. Indeed, he only failed them once when he had to attend urgent business at his office in Hay. Somehow or other, with the help of Sampson, he managed to keep his business afloat. Similarly, across the road, the offices of Robert Griffiths were also struggling to survive. The old gentleman was far from well and his son, Trevor, set to succeed him, had been forced to suspend his legal duties to serve in France.

It is possible that Armstrong, despite his age, may have welcomed army life and probably enjoyed the camaraderie, deference to rank and the freedom to enjoy a drink and a smoke, two pleasures strictly monitored at home.

In 1916, he was promoted to the rank of Major and later served the last three months of the war in France. Katharine worried constantly about him and, fearful that he might be killed in action, made a will on 17 January, 1917, naming the children—a third child, Margaret, was born in that year—the main beneficiaries. But Armstrong was fortunate to survive the war, finally returning to England in October 1918. Though officially retired from the army in 1921 he chose to retain his title of Major in civilian life. It was a matter of considerable pride and he became a familiar sight striding through the narrow streets of Hay wearing riding breeches and his Cavalry coat with the collar turned up, sometimes carrying a swagger stick, still very much a military man.

Once Katharine and the children were back at Mayfield Armstrong set to work to save his business by consolidating the clients he had left behind and attracting more. By that time the other solicitor, Robert Griffiths, had, in the absence of his son, Trevor, taken on a new man, one Oswald Norman Martin, the man who was to play a devastating role in the downfall of Major Armstrong. Oswald Martin was a 30 year old bachelor who, having been wounded in the jaw, had been invalided out of the army. This injury had resulted in a partial paralysis of the right side of his face which, in turn, caused him to have a quite discernible speech impediment. Originally from Tewkesbury, in Gloucestershire, where his brother was in the retail grocery business, he soon settled into Griffiths's office in Broad Street and it was here that he met Constance Davies, daughter of Fred Davies, the chemist. She had been a nurse at the beginning of the war but ended up entertaining the troops in France. After the war, Constance had been employed as a typist by Robert Griffiths and, within weeks of her introduction to Oswald Martin, they became engaged to be married.

Some writers on the case have suggested that Armstrong felt threatened by the arrival of Oswald Martin but in fact the reverse may have been true. Armstrong had always known that either Robert Griffiths's son, or one or other of the hundreds of young solicitors looking for work after demobilization, would one day join the other firm. Furthermore, far from attracting clients, Martin's presence across the road was, in fact, deflecting a number of Robert Griffiths's older clients who preferred to deal with an established solicitor like Armstrong who was well known and trusted locally, rather than with a relative youngster who was new to the area.

There was also something about Martin that put people off, a certain flashiness, perhaps, for in photographs he can be seen sporting a floppy bow-tie, definitely not one of the pinstripe or cavalry twill brigade. As for Constance, after their marriage she took to wearing luxuriant fox furs, not just one but several layers of full pelts. This manner of dress, though very much in vogue for city dwellers, may have seemed a trifle theatrical for a typist in a small market town like Hay.

As to inappropriate dress, Mrs Armstrong had firm views on that score. Not long after his engagement Oswald Martin received a formal invitation to tea at Mayfield. Two other guests, an army officer and his wife, had also been invited and Katharine was horrified when Martin arrived casually dressed in flannels and sports jacket. It is difficult now to fully appreciate the emphasis ladies like Katharine Armstrong placed on traditional ceremonies like taking afternoon tea and being dressed accordingly. She was deeply offended by this breach of the dress code and Armstrong said later that 'Martin was never invited to the house again so long as my wife was alive'.

This incident and Katharine's exaggerated reaction illustrates the demarcation within the class system in Hay in the 1920s—it was clearly a case of knowing the class into which one was born and staying in it. By marrying a solicitor, Constance Davies and her family may have thought they could cross that invisible line between tradespeople and the professional class. What they did not realise was that Oswald Martin, despite his professional position was still, in the eyes of some, 'in trade' like his brother and father-in-law.

It would appear that Fred Davies, in particular, felt this very keenly. He professed dislike for Armstrong and resented the fact that he had acted for another chemist, Mr Sant, when he set up a rival pharmacy in the town, which, although not licensed to dispense medicines, was proving very popular. Judged by his photographs, Davies seems to have been rather a sour-faced and insular man: yet he saw himself as somebody in the town, a man of substance and a force to be reckoned with—he was, after all, a qualified chemist who had worked in Hay for forty years, dispensed his own medicines and had been, like Armstrong, a Freemason. Yet he sensed he was still not accepted on an equal footing socially, and he resented it bitterly.

During the war, Jay, the gardener at Mayfield, had done his best to control the weeds by once again using patent weedkillers but when the Major returned he was exasperated to see how overgrown the garden had become in his absence. The paths and especially the driveway were once more completely smothered with dandelions. He now renewed his battle, determined to eradicate the weeds once and for all. In June, 1919, intent once more on using his special recipe he bought half a pound of arsenic and some caustic soda from Fred Davies's shop and, once again, signed the Sale of Poisons Book. He used half of this packet and put the remainder in a tin next to the caustic soda in the cupboard in the study.

Despite the weed problem, life seemed, at least, a little brighter. The country, no longer at war, had begun to recover from its gloom; there was a new optimism and Armstrong was happy to be back in the fold of his family. His eldest child, Eleanor, was now 11 years old and attending a boarding school in Malvern whilst Katharine taught Pearson at home, giving him lessons in the study every morning. The youngest child, Margaret, was now a bright, vivacious 4 year old, and a great favourite with everyone.

As for Katharine, she supervised her household, entertained selected neighbours to tea, involved herself in church matters and tended the roses. She read a great deal and enjoyed playing the piano for her family and guests. But like many women raised in excessively religious families, with its stultifying atmosphere of repression, Katharine was prone to periods of self-loathing, doubt and recrimination. At times she could be strong-willed, dogmatic and acutely introspective, yet she was easily excited, demonstrating her nervousness in frenetic chattering.

She had also become a hypochondriac and, having little faith in doctors, continued to dose herself with a veritable arsenal of homeopathic remedies. But when, in 1919, she developed pains in her right shoulder and arm, accompanied by some numbness in her fingers, she was sufficiently worried to consult Dr Hincks. His surgery was in Broad Street, close to the Town Clock and just up the road from her husband's office. Tom Hincks was a large, country-squire type of man and was, as his father before him, extremely popular. People trusted Hincks and regularly converged on his surgery, especially on market days. Harassed mothers would come in from the outlying farms with their menfolk and livestock, dragging along their sickly brood— some with rickets, some with hacking coughs, others with scabies and squints and all manner of complaints, convinced that if anyone could sort them out, Tom Hincks could. Whether he was, in fact, wholly competent at diagnosing disease is debatable but he was certainly a hard-working man, in the saddle for many hours each week visiting patients living in the more inaccessible hill farms around Hay.

Knowing that Mrs Armstrong had a history of rheumatism Hincks diagnosed and treated her for brachial neuritis, and although the condition gradually improved she was rarely completely free of its effects.

It was in July the following year that Armstrong alleged that Katharine made a new will, leaving the bulk of her estate to him. This will was, in fact, invalid for it was written in Armstrong's hand and, it was later proved, his wife's signature was a forgery. When subsequently questioned about this Armstrong explained that as his wife's rheumatic condition made writing difficult he had done it for her—not an entirely plausible explanation, it must be said, for a solicitor to make—yet Katharine seems to have been fully compliant with the arrangement for Miss Pearce later testified that when she was called to witness the document she signed her name in the presence of both Mr and Mrs Armstrong. However, the second witness, the young maid, Lily Candy, was not present. When questioned she insisted that she signed the document in the library at Mayfield on a quite different occasion, when only Major Armstrong was present.

In the meantime, about a month after the signing of the will, in August, 1920, Katharine began to feel unwell. She was under considerable stress having to cope with all three children at home for the summer holidays without the help of Miss Pearce who had taken a month's leave. It was all too much for her and she cracked under the strain, becoming deluded and depressed.

Armstrong, worried by his wife's irrational behaviour and restlessness at night—she had taken to wandering about downstairs, imagining people outside were staring at her through the windows—asked Dr Hincks to prescribe a sleeping draught for her. He brought her a gift of a bunch of violets and did everything he could for her, even asking his elder daughter, Eleanor, to observe her carefully during the day and report back to him in the evenings. But Katharine did not improve and on a subsequent visit to Mayfield on 20 August, Dr Hincks could see that Katharine was not being simply neurotic but was suffering from a serious mental disturbance. On examination he detected a mitral murmur of the heart and, having taken a urine sample, found traces of albumen, usually a symptom of underlying kidney damage or disease. (It was later suggested that Katharine may have been suffering from Addison's disease.)

The following day Armstrong sent for his wife's sister, Bessie, and their old friend, Arthur Chevalier. There was a family conference during which Dr Hincks suggested that Katharine should be admitted to a private asylum, Barnwood House, near Gloucester, where his own sister had recently been treated. It was also agreed that, as Katharine was a potential suicide risk, the Major's razors and service revolver should be securely stored. In Hincks's opinion, Katharine's condition was probably due to the menopause; she was, after all, now aged 47 and of a nervous, melancholic disposition. Dr Jayne, from Talgarth, was called to give a second opinion and found Katharine distressed and rambling and suffering from the delusion that she had lived an ungodly life, had treated her children cruelly and had frequently defrauded the tradesmen. After further discussion with the family it was decided that Katharine should be certified insane.

Whilst Katharine was at Barnwood she was treated for a month with a tonic containing arsenic and slowly improved. Armstrong visited her every two weeks as advised by the hospital doctor, and on each occasion Katharine begged her husband to take her home for she hated Barnwood and missed her children dreadfully.

Winter that year had been particularly wet and mild. Armstrong, probably intending to get the place tidied up before his wife's home-coming, and forgetting that he already had some arsenic left over in the cupboard, bought another quarter pound from Fred Davies's shop on 11 January. He said later it had been his intention to use it that weekend but, feeling unwell and confined to bed, he had put it away in the cupboard, still wrapped and tied with string. (Although it was never established that Major Armstrong had the disease, Dr Hincks was treating him with a course of painful mercury injections for *suspected* syphilis at the time.) Armstrong placed the arsenic on top of the tin of caustic soda, unopened and therefore unaware that John Hird, the chemist's assistant, had inadvertently sold him white arsenic, having forgotten to tint it as before with charcoal.

By 22 January, 1921, five months after her admission, the doctor at Barnwood reluctantly agreed that Katharine had improved sufficiently to be allowed to go home in the care of her husband and a local nurse, Gladys Kinsey, though he felt the move a little premature. He was soon proved right—she continued suffering delusions, was physically weak and so depressed that at times she appeared to harbour thoughts of suicide. In fact, soon after her return, she asked the nurse whether a fall from the attic window would be sufficient to kill someone. So convinced did Gladys become that Katharine would try to commit suicide that she asked the Major if he could send for a properly trained psychiatric nurse. Equally concerned for his wife's health, he obtained the services of Eva Allen from Cardiff. In addition he told the maids to be especially vigilant.

On 8 February, Mrs Armstrong celebrated her 48th birthday, which was to be her last. On 13 February, after eating Sunday lunch of mutton followed by bottled gooseberries with the rest of the family, she was sick. The following day a neighbour called to see Katharine and saw her sitting on the veranda, wrapped in a shawl and obviously unwell.

On 16 February, Katharine had given Pearson his usual lesson in the study (during which she had become annoyed at having to waste time looking for his lost exercise book) but after lunch she was again taken ill, complaining of acute dyspepsia. The previous day, Nurse Allen had taken away the homeopathic pills Katharine had been accustomed to taking for indigestion, instead, she had given her some bicarbonate in water. She tried this again and found some temporary relief but when her condition worsened Armstrong sent for Dr Hincks. On examination he found that Katharine's skin was discoloured and, after she suffered a bout of severe vomiting, he declared that she was 'very acutely ill'.

Hincks then visited daily but Katharine's condition continued to deteriorate. Subject to continual vomiting she became emaciated and spent most of her time in bed. Just how mobile Katharine was during the last six days of her life was to become a point of crucial importance. She kept most, if not all, her homeopathic medicines in a small, unlocked chest on the mantelshelf, about three or four feet from her bed. Both Dr Hincks and Nurse Allen knew that Katharine was taking her own medication but after a cursory check on 15 February, neither bothered to inspect the medicine chest or monitor what their patient was taking. The nurse later confirmed that Katharine had continued using her own medicines right up until Monday 21 February, by which time she was very seriously ill and, by all accounts, too weak to get out of bed. On that morning Nurse Allen left her for at least an hour while she walked to Dr Hincks's surgery in Hay to fetch some nutrient suppositories.

After a restless night in the care of a relief nurse, it was clear that Mrs Armstrong was dying. By nine o'clock in the morning, after a brief conversation with her husband, she lost consciousness. Unable to help in any way and led to believe by Dr Hincks that she could last the rest of the day, Armstrong accepted the offer of a lift into Hay to catch up on some work. Katharine Armstrong died a few minutes after he reached his office.

The funeral, on Friday 25 February, at St Mary's, Cusop, was a small affair attended by Bessie Friend, Arthur Chevalier and a few close friends. The wording on the wreath from Major Armstrong and his children read: 'From Herbert and the Chicks'.

In the month following his bereavement Armstrong became ill and depressed. Amongst others, he received a letter of sympathy from a long-time friend, Marion Gale, a kindly, middle-aged widow who, with her elderly mother, had befriended Armstrong when he was stationed in the West Country during the war. Before taking the advice of Dr Hincks to take a short holiday in Sicily, he saw Marion during a business trip to London. In May that year he asked her to marry him, spurred on, perhaps, not from any great passion but rather the need to find a sympathetic companion and housekeeper who would help share the burden of raising his three young children.

While Marion considered his proposal Mayfield remained empty during the early summer of that year. With the children still at school and Miss Pearce on holiday it was a lonely time for the Major; he went to stay with his neighbours across the road, Mr and Mrs Tunnard Moore. It was at this time that he decided to tackle the dandelions once more, using the arsenic he'd bought in January that year. Taking advantage of the children's absence, he went over to Mayfield and proceeded to make a score or more sachets, each containing a few grains of arsenic. He said later that it was only at this point, when he opened the packet in the cupboard, that he realised that he had been sold *white* arsenic. He said he also noticed that the string, which had been secure when he put the packet away, had been untied. Unaware of any significance in this and not wishing to create trouble for Fred Davies's assistant, he said nothing.

Armed with the little packets, and using an old chisel to make an incision into the roots of the most stubborn weeds, he dropped the arsenic directly into the hole he'd made, thus killing the weed at the root without damaging the surrounding grass. He spent the afternoon happily killing off weeds, at the end of which he was unaware that there was one sachet left amongst the other bits and pieces in the pocket of his gardening jacket. As he had only used half the arsenic he placed the remaining two ounces, still in the original paper, in a drawer in his bureau.

Having had to cope with the loss of his wife and organise the children's schooling it was time for Armstrong to settle down to business once more. He and Oswald Martin were soon to cross swords over a land purchasing deal, one of some duration and complexity. This involved the sale of a mansion known as Velinewydd and a number of tenanted farms, on behalf of the owner for whom Armstrong was acting. These had been offered by auction at Brecon, the sale being interrupted by the angry tenant farmers, Martin's clients, violently opposed to the sales. Eventually, matters reached a point where the contracts on the sales were withdrawn and the return of the deposits demanded. Despite this, the two men remained on fairly cordial terms— Martin would occasionally borrow books from Armstrong's excellent library and always maintained that he found the latter courteous and helpful. Nevertheless, he professed to be a little surprised when, at the height of the conflict over the contract, Armstrong invited him to tea at Mayfield on Wednesday, 26 October. Armstrong, despite his Masonic and business matters, was still lonely after his wife's death and often invited visitors to his home in the evenings. The meal, consisting of a pot of tea, scones and currant bread, had been prepared by the housekeeper, Miss Pearce, and, after a stroll round the garden, the two men ate in the drawing room.

Martin later insisted that Armstrong passed him a buttered scone with the words, 'Excuse my fingers'. Miss Pearce, however, who baked the scones, and Harriet Price, who served the tea, said that the scones were uncut and unbuttered. Martin was surprised, as he tucked into several slices of buttered currant loaf, that Armstrong didn't bring up the business of the Velinewydd sale, as he assumed this was the reason for his invitation to Mayfield. Instead, the two men talked generally about the pressure of work and staff shortages before parting at six-thirty.

Later that evening, after eating supper of jugged rabbit and crême caramel with his wife, Martin was taken ill with severe pains in his stomach and prolonged bouts of vomiting. When called, Dr Hincks diagnosed a bilious attack brought on by overwork and lack of exercise and prescribed bismuth.

The following morning, however, Fred Davies, discussing his son-in-law's illness with Dr Hincks said that, in his opinion, Martin had been poisoned. It must be remembered that less than eighteen months before, another solicitor, Harold Greenwood, from Kidwelly, near Carmarthen, had been tried and acquitted of the murder of his wife with arsenic. The case, which had been widely reported in the press, had become a favourite topic of conversation in Hay. The verdict was generally regarded with scepticism and there can be little doubt that the case had done much to fuel Davies's suspicions concerning the death of Mrs Armstrong.

So convinced was he that she had been poisoned and so virulent was his animus towards his son-in-law's rival that he couldn't resist telling Hincks of his suspicions. The doctor was initially reluctant to go along with this startling suggestion and continued to treat Martin for a bilious attack.

But then, on 30 October, Davies suddenly produced a box of chocolates— two of which showed signs of being tampered with—and told Dr Hincks that the chocolates had been sent anonymously through the post to Oswald Martin on 20 September. The sender, Davies was sure, was Major Armstrong. Martin and his wife had eaten a couple of the chocolates and then put the box away until they gave a small dinner party on 8 October. One of their guests that evening was Martin's sister, Dorothy: she had eaten one of the chocolates and later that night, according to Davies, had been taken very ill with vomiting and diarrhoea.

Taking into account the two incidence of sickness, Hincks agreed to take a sample of Martin's urine for analysis. This was done the following day, under far from sterile conditions. Davies produced an empty bottle, which had contained hydrogen peroxide, from a cupboard in his dispensary, and Martin's urine sample, along with the suspect chocolates, were parcelled up and sent to the Clinical Research Association in London.

The analysis, made for the Home Office by Dr John Webster, established that there were traces of arsenic in the urine sample and in two of the chocolates. On the strength of these results the Director of Prosecutions ordered an immediate investigation which culminated two months later in the arrest of Major Armstrong on a charge of attempted murder of Oswald Martin.

The arrest was made at Armstrong's office shortly after ten o'clock on Saturday, 31 December, 1921, by Albert Weaver, Deputy Chief Constable of Herefordshire and Chief Inspector Alfred Crutchett of New Scotland Yard. Shocked but co-operative, Armstrong made a voluntary written statement and even offered to accompany the police officers to Mayfield where he said he would show them where to find his stock of arsenic. It was at this point that a fatal mistake was made—he forgot about the remaining two ounces of the white arsenic which he had put in the drawer of the bureau. It was only when, a little later, he was formally arrested and asked to turn out his pockets of his gardening jacket and saw the small packet of arsenic left over from his last attack on the dandelions, that he remembered the arsenic in the bureau. He also realised that the police would find it there but, having initially omitted to mention it, saw that he was in a very awkward position. He did the only thing possible—he told his solicitor, T.A. Matthews.

Detective Chief Constable Weaver leads Major Armstrong
into the Hay Courthouse

The magistrates at Hay

To further compound the dilemma the police made two subsequent searches at Mayfield but failed to find the white arsenic and it was only on Matthews's second visit, in the company of Dr Ainslie, that the arsenic was found, wedged in the back of a drawer. Expecting the police to find it eventually, Matthews decided, perhaps with hindsight, unwisely, to put it back in the bureau and say nothing.

On the following Monday morning Armstrong had to bear the shame of appearing in the tiny courthouse in Hay, where he was still officially Clerk to the Magistrates. On hearing the charge against him his manner remained calm; he even went out of his way to help the elderly gentleman who had replaced him as clerk. He stood to attention when charged, neatly dressed and sporting a bright red tie for the occasion. He was remanded in custody pending further investigations, no doubt painfully aware that news of his arrest had probably already spread throughout the town. It had—and as he was escorted from the building there were cheers of support and someone called out: 'Three cheers for the Major!'

Dr Hincks, at first unwilling to share Fred Davies's suspicions about Armstrong, now turned against him. He told police that he thought Katharine

Armstrong had died, not of gastro-enteritis, but from arsenical poisoning. An order was obtained on 2 January for the exhumation of her body which was examined by Bernard Spilsbury, considered to be the most experienced pathologist of the day. The corpse was taken from the churchyard of St Mary's to nearby Church Cottage where the windows had been boarded up to frustrate the ghoulish attentions of the onlookers. But little could be seen for it was already dark and Humphrey Webb, the undertaker, and his son had to work by lantern light. A young lad was sent down to Hay for a bottle of whisky to fortify the men in their grisly work and on his return he happened to see into the room where the body had been laid out on wooden trestles. He was shocked to see that Mrs Armstrong was still recognisable nearly a year after her burial, even down to the bows of ribbon on the end of her plaited hair. (The presence of arsenic in a body, whether ingested or through seepage or migration from surrounding soil, can act as a preservative.)

A detailed analysis of specimens taken from the body showed that, as Fred Davies had suspected, there was arsenic in virtually every part of Katharine Armstrong's body, more than nine and a half grains, and it was deemed that her husband, now on remand in Worcester Gaol, was responsible.

At the resumed Magistrates' hearing in the little courthouse at Hay, Armstrong was further charged with the murder of his wife. Having heard the testimony of a number of witnesses the magistrates decided that there was a case to answer and ordered that Armstrong stand trial at the next Hereford Assizes for the murder of his wife and the attempted murder of Oswald Martin.

The presiding judge was 73 year old Mr Justice Darling, a controversial figure, considered a wit with literary aspirations. It was to be his last murder case before his retirement and from the outset he seemed determined to secure a conviction. As in all major poison cases the role of prosecutor was taken by the Attorney General, in this instance, Sir Ernest Pollock. He was assisted by a formidable medical team—in addition to Bernard Spilsbury, there were Sir William Wilcox, physician and Dr John Webster, Senior Analyst at the Home Office, all considered experts in their field.

Defending Armstrong against this prestigious panel was Sir Henry Curtis Bennett, KC. Whilst undoubtedly an imposing figure and a most able advocate, he lacked the fire and dramatic impact of Marshall Hall, the successful defender of Greenwood at Carmarthen, who had been approached as defence counsel for Armstrong but was unwell and unable to accept the brief. Curtis Bennett was backed by three excellent but far from eminent physicians—Drs Toogood, Stead and Ainslie.

The trial, which opened on 3 April, 1922, at the Shire Hall in Hereford, lasted for ten days and excited immense interest, not just locally but nationally. Despite the harsh weather—there had been a recent fall of snow—vast crowds gathered outside the court to watch the daily comings and goings of the legal dignitaries and, of course, to catch a glimpse of Major Armstrong. For the occasion he was wearing his brown tweed suit, spats and brown boots, and his moustache was elegantly waxed.

The first charge related to the murder of Katharine Armstrong and the judge, despite the adamant objection of Curtis Bennett, ruled that the evidence relating to the second charge of attempted murder of Oswald Martin should be admissable. This evidence, Curtis Bennett was sure, though purely circumstantial, would prove highly prejudical to Armstrong. (A third charge, of attempting to murder Oswald Martin by poisoned chocolates, had earlier been dismissed through lack of evidence though the jurors must have known about the chocolates, if only from newspaper articles.)

A close study of the trial shows that Mr Justice Darling was quite openly biased in favour of the prosecution. He conspicuously elevated the testimony of the Home Office experts with sycophantic introductions whilst doing his utmost to belittle the defence doctors by his disparaging comments throughout the proceedings. He openly ridiculed Armstrong's defence and towards the end of the trial, when the cross-examination was complete—and, it must be said, when the case for the defence looked most plausible—he ordered Armstrong to remain in the witness box and proceeded to submit him to an onslaught of invective. He questioned him unremittingly about the white arsenic in the bureau and about the little packet found in his coat pocket. It was during this interrogation that Armstrong, having previously taken the stand for nearly six hours and answered questions with calm courtesy, began to show signs of stress. He seemed to lose his customary confidence, become almost inarticulate and his answers lacked conviction. When he was finally allowed to leave the witness box the damage to his credibility was irreparable.

In his summing up, Mr Justice Darling strongly recommended the jury to accept the prosecution's view that Katharine Armstrong was being slowly poisoned before she went to Barnwood and that the final dose of arsenic must have been given to her within twenty-four hours of her death—at a time when she was supposedly incapable of taking it herself. He dismissed entirely the theory proposed by the defence doctors that all the symptoms presented by Mrs Armstrong before she went to Barnwood were due to auto-intoxication—an accumulation of 'natural' poisons that had built up in her body, producing symptoms such as constipation, neuritis, rheumatoid arthritis and chronic indigestion and possibly also causing the albumen in her urine and the condition of her heart. The judge failed to address the fact that if Mrs Armstrong had already been criminally poisoned the use of a tonic containing arsenic in the asylum would have caused her condition to deteriorate, not, as it had, improve.

Convinced that Katharine had been suicidal, the defence doctors had suggested that she had taken a large dose of arsenic some days before her death, some of which had become encapsulated and attached itself to mucous in the wall of the stomach and so not been immediately absorbed by the body. They explained this to the jury, describing how arsenic, like most poisons, was capricious by nature and variable in its effects. Indeed, although a minimum fatal dose was generally acknowledged to be between two or three grains there had been many recorded cases of patients living for several days after taking massive doses. It was the opinion of the defence that the duration of Katharine Armstrong's last illness would suggest that, having taken a fairly large dose, part had become encapsulated, later to dissolve and pass down into the bowel, ultimately causing her death.

As to the three-hundredths of a grain of arsenic found in Oswald Martin's urine, the defence reminded the jury that Martin had been taking bismuth for four or five days prior to giving the urine sample. Bismuth was notoriously susceptible to arsenic contamination, a point not contested by the Crown. In addition, the urine sample was taken in an amateurish manner and in far from sterile conditions—the bottle used, for instance, had previously contained hydrogen peroxide, a substance known to harbour arsenical impurities. Furthermore, urged the defence, the bottle had been stored in a cupboard in Davies's dispensary alongside a number of other bottles, some of which could have contained noxious substances. These perfectly valid points were derided by the judge in his summing up and the jury were left in little doubt as to where his own convictions lay.

At various times, whilst listening to Darling's closing speech, which lasted four hours, Armstrong, according to a local reporter, was seen to be balancing a copy of the Bible—on which he had sworn before giving evidence—on its spine along the front of the dock, and catching it each time just as it was about to fall.

At the start of the trial Curtis Bennett had been absolutely convinced that, when dealing with the murder charge, the evidence concerning the tea-party at Mayfield was inadmissable. He therefore conducted, erroneously in retrospect, a purely passive defence, content that the Crown could not prove beyond a reasonable doubt that Armstrong had given arsenic to his wife. One cannot help feeling that had Marshall Hall conducted the defence the jury could probably have been convinced that Katharine did take a fatal dose of white arsenic herself, either accidentally, mistaking it for bicarbonate of soda, or with the clear intention of taking her own life. She was, after all, depressed, fearful and very confused at the time.

The jurors left the court to consider their verdict at eight minutes to five in the afternoon. So confident was Curtis Bennett of an acquittal, despite the judge's behaviour, that he went for a walk only to be told that the jury, after just forty minutes' deliberation, had returned a verdict of guilty. He was absolutely shattered by his defeat. He told a reporter: 'I have been in forty-eight murder trials, for and against, and I have never known the verdict so open'. He later referred to the trial as 'unjust' and a 'poor show'.

It came as no surprise, however, that Mr Justice Darling told the stunned court that he totally concurred with the verdict and renounced any suggestion that Katharine Armstrong had committed suicide. Telling Armstrong that he had been given 'a fair trial' and been 'brilliantly defended' he proceeded to sentence him to death.

Afterwards, the foreman of the jury told the press that they had convicted Armstrong on the grounds that firstly, they accepted the prosecution's view that Katharine Armstrong had been given the arsenic within twenty-four hours of her death and secondly, they did not believe the Major's explanation for the presence of the little packet of arsenic in his pocket at the time of his arrest. Huge crowds of onlookers and reporters, many of whom were convinced of Armstrong's innocence, and therefore shocked and angered by the guilty verdict, watched in silence as the car took him back to Gloucester Gaol. One reporter noticed that the Major, huddled in the back seat, was quietly weeping.

Curtis Bennett was not the only one to be devastated by the verdict. So, too, was Tom Matthews who had worked tirelessly in Armstrong's defence. He received numerous letters of support, including many from gardeners willing to testify that they used similar devices to Armstrong to kill off individual weeds. Various newspapers and journals took up the argument and many expressed dissatisfaction, not only with the verdict, but with many aspects of the trial—in particular, the blatant bias of the judge. The popular crime writer, Edgar Wallace, protested angrily in an article published in *John Bull* on 15 April, saying that there was nothing odd about a man going to the trouble of killing the roots of individual weeds with arsenic. 'I knew a man in Africa,' he wrote, 'who used to carry a little phial of nicotine to destroy certain flies that pestered his roses. If some of us,' he went on, 'were on trial for our lives and our eccentricities were produced against us, I daresay that they would seem even more absurd than Armstrong's'.

Harold Greenwood also wrote an emotive article in the following week's issue of the same magazine in which he commiserated with the fate of Armstrong. His sincerity, however, was a little suspect, for he also wrote several unpleasantly avaricious letters to Armstrong himself, trying to act as broker for a newspaper that wanted to publish an article written by Armstrong as he awaited execution.

But an appeal was lodged and during the hearing, which lasted three days, Curtis Bennett, in a last desperate attempt to save his client, spoke for twelve hours. He vehemently protested against the admissibility of the Oswald Martin evidence and demanded that the guilty verdict should be quashed. The appeal was dismissed on 16 May and the sentence of death remained.

The warders who were with Armstrong during his last days found him to be a man of courage and courtesy and one deeply concerned for his children. His last hours were spent in writing letters of thanks to his friend and solicitor, Tom Matthews, and also to Rev J.J. de Winton, vicar of Hay, who were both convinced of his innocence. He made all the necessary arrangements for the care of his children, nominating Arthur Chevalier as their legal guardian. He also bestowed various small gifts to those who had been kind to him throughout his ordeal.

Herbert Rowse Armstrong was hanged at Gloucester Gaol on 31 May, 1922, at eight in the morning. Thousands had signed a petition for a reprieve and such was the interest in the case that a vast crowd had gathered. So slight was Armstrong's frame that John Ellis, the public executioner, provided an extra long drop of eight feet eight inches to ensure there was sufficient pull on the rope to dislocate his neck. Armstrong maintained his innocence to the end but accepted his fate and walked to the scaffold unaided.

That Katharine Armstrong died of arsenical poisoning there can be no doubt but the central question is whether Armstrong gave it to her or she took it herself. Armstrong was convicted on purely circumstantial evidence for no person saw him give his wife arsenic. He bought the arsenic quite openly, unlike most known poisoners, and as for trying to poison Oswald Martin, surely he would not have used poison bought from his intended victim's father-in-law, a shrewd and suspicious man who already disliked him intensely?

More significantly, knowing the outcome of the Greenwood case in which the exhumation of Mabel Greenwood's body led to her husband's arrest for murder, surely Armstrong, if he had poisoned Katharine, would have taken the

extra precaution of having her body cremated, or at least not created additional risk of discovery by attempting a second murder? It is worth noting
when considering this case that the hallmark of a clever poisoner is to isolate
the intended victim from his or her family and limit medical intervention as
much as possible. Armstrong did neither—in fact, quite the reverse. As soon
as Katharine became ill he sent for her sister and a close family friend and
pestered Dr Hincks to come to the house every day to monitor her illness. He
even employed a full-time psychiatric nurse to care for her and urged the
whole household to be more vigilant. It is also remarkable that, after
Katharine's death, Armstrong, if he had something to hide, did not at once
insinuate that she had committed suicide. In the circumstances, this would
have been accepted as a sad, but wholly plausible outcome of Katharine's
tragic decline into depression and mental instability.

And what of motive? The Major had not touched the small amount of
money he inherited from Katharine's will and as for his relationship with
Marion Gale, even Mr Justice Darling was unable to suggest it was anything
other than friendship at the time of Katharine's death. Were the case to come
before a jury today it would probably decide that the purely circumstantial
evidence was insufficient to prove beyond a reasonable doubt that Armstrong
killed his wife. On the balance of probability, taking into account Mrs
Armstrong's medical history, it is possible that she took the arsenic herself,
either by accident or intent. She had little faith in conventional medicine and
none whatever in Dr Hincks. Not only did she doubt his diagnostic skills she
was also fearful of being returned to the asylum. The nurse was well aware
that she was taking her own medicines right up until the day before she died.
She regularly left Katharine for half an hour while she had her lunch and occasionally during the afternoon when she took a walk. Sometimes, but by no
means on every occasion, the maid, Inez Rosser, was sent to sit with Mrs
Armstrong during the nurse's absence.

On the morning of 21 February, Nurse Allen left her to walk to Dr Hincks's
surgery in Hay which must have taken her at least an hour, there and back.
Was it then that Katharine, desperate to get better, took the arsenic that killed
her? At Barnwood, she had been given a tonic containing arsenic and her
condition had improved. She knew there was arsenic in the cupboard in the
study. Did she come across it on the morning she was taken ill, whilst
searching for Sonny's book? And did she take some up to her room that day,
keeping a secret supply under her pillow or in the medicine chest close to her
bed? Had she, perhaps, since her return to Mayfield, been dosing herself with

little pinches of arsenic as a tonic? The postmortem findings certainly pointed to repeated small doses in the weeks before her death. Knowing she was losing control and fearful of being returned to Barnwood did she panic and take a larger dose? Did she take it deliberately or did she confuse it with one of her special homeopathic powders, or take a pinch of white arsenic, accidentally mistaking it for bicarbonate of soda, which the nurse had given her when she was bilious? There were, after all, numerous bottles, boxes and sachets crammed into the medicine chest—a confusing array for someone as mentally disturbed as Katharine undoubtedly was at the time.

The idea that she may have stored some of the arsenic in one of her own homeopathic medicine bottles is given credence by her daughter, Eleanor. Though too young to testify at her father's trial, she nevertheless confided in a neighbour, Mary Tunnard Moore, saying: 'When Mummy was so ill she told me to be very careful with the bottles, because if she took the wrong one and anything happened, Daddy would be blamed'.

Unfortunately, it is never possible in a case such as this to know what really happened, how this particular tragedy came about so long ago. Or explain why, even now, the little Major continues to hold such a particular fascination for criminologists. A man, very much of his time, a true Edwardian, dutiful, resourceful and diligent whose life, by his own admission, centred on his family and work. A man who, until his arrest, had led an unremarkable life, elevated only by the stoicism with which he met his death—an infamous death which may have been brought about, not by the crime of murder at all, but by fate and the ill-concealed malice in other men's hearts.

Fred Davies and Oswald Martin left Hay soon after Armstrong's execution. Martin died in 1946, aged 56. Marion Gale died in 1960, aged 91, and Dr Tom Hincks died at 57, of a heart attack whilst riding in the fields behind Armstrong's former home, Mayfield, in 1932. The 'poisoned chocolates' were kept by Sir William Wilcox and frequently exhibited during his lectures on toxicology at St Mary's Hospital, London.

There are some people in Hay who still cannot believe in Armstrong's guilt and remember him for his many acts of kindness, especially to the unemployed he encountered during the stringent post-war years. The old police station and the cell in which Armstrong was kept immediately after his arrest—and where he played chess with the warders for hours on end—are now part of a private dwelling. By coincidence, it is now the home of Bob Knights and, until her recent death, his wife, Marina, who was related to Inez Rosser, the young maid who was employed in the Armstrong household.

Evidently, the girl had liked the Major, and spoken well of him to her family, saying that his behaviour towards her had always been that of a perfect gentleman. Mrs Knights's father had served with Major Armstrong in the army and also remembered him with respect and affection, commenting on his quiet, kindly voice. The old Magistrates Court has since been converted to a domestic residence.

The firm of solicitors for whom Oswald Martin worked, now Gabb & Co, still operates from the same premises on the corner of Chancery Lane and Broad Street and across the road are the offices of Major Armstrong's former practice, now Williams Beales & Co. The brass plate bearing Armstrong's name remains in its place on the office wall. By a series of coincidences, the firm is now owned by Martin Beales, who at one time lived with his young family in Church Cottage, Cusop, where Mrs Armstrong's exhumed body was examined. And now, by a further twist of fate, they live in Major Armstrong's former home, Mayfield, re-named, The Mantles. It is a now a charming family home of great warmth and ease and the sad history of the house and the tragic Armstrong family has, it seems, been laid to rest.

Martin Beales's book, *Dead not Buried* (which was awarded the Crime Writers' Association Gold Dagger Award) was published in 1995 and in that same year, to the astonishment of the audience, Armstrong's daughter, Margaret, made a surprise appearance at the Hay Festival of Literature, prior to a discussion on stage between Beales and a previous writer on the case, Robin Odell.

*　*　*　*　*

Two years after Major Armstrong's execution there was another tragedy in Hay but unlike the Armstrong case, which gained world-wide publicity, it has remained a private grief. It concerned the death of Rose Williams, wife of a farmer in the Llanbedr hills and a mother of six children. One Thursday, shortly before Christmas, she left the market in Hay on horseback, the panniers on either side of the saddle heavily laden with the goods she had bought that day. As she crossed Hay bridge the snow was already falling steadily so she urged the pony onwards up the hill towards home.

By the time she reached the village of Clyro, a fierce blizzard had set in and the roads were already becoming treacherous. Some of the villagers gave her a hot drink and begged her to stay overnight but she said that her children would be waiting for her and insisted on going on, determined to reach home by nightfall. She never did reach home. She was found frozen to death on the hills beyond Painscastle.

CHAPTER 8

Hay Against Hitler

By 1940, Hay, like the rest of Britain, was steeped in the grey, austere gloom of the war years. Many of the town's young men had been conscripted into the armed forces and were already in action, though as farmers were needed to maintain the nation's vital food supply, many others were exempt. Wireless and newspaper reports were constantly urging people to support the War Effort, either by volunteering for Civil Defence duties or taking on the jobs normally done by the conscripted men. The elderly, youngsters without skills, indeed everybody, was encouraged to do something. Women were, as usual, surprisingly resilient and rose to the occasion. Whilst some underwent emergency training in First Aid with the Red Cross others joined the Land Army, manned the Fire Stations, worked in the munitions factories or drove ambulances, buses and delivery trucks. Gladys Morgan, as she was then, became a replacement 'chippie' on the bus from Hay to Brecon for five years until, that is, the conductor returned from active service.

Many of the men and women from Hay and district commuted daily to the munitions factory in Hereford throughout the war years, working one of three shifts which they called the Red, White and Blue. Those on the first shift, six in the morning until two in the afternoon, had to get up at four and catch a special bus that left Hay at ten to five. During hours of darkness, when the black-out was in force, the bus travelled between Hay and Hereford with the vehicle's headlights covered with peaked hoods, cut with slits, through which the light was beamed directly on to the road but was virtually invisible from above. Once they reached the factory the women had to change into special fire-proof clothing and were forbidden to wear hair-grips or jewellery of any kind, not even their wedding rings for fear of generating sparks. The work was both tedious and potentially dangerous and out of their wages of £2 for a six day week they spent 2 shillings and 6 pence on their bus fares.

Every conceivable effort was made to keep the country on its feet and thwart the enemy. Ladies who were either too old or too frail to tackle such heavy duties picked up their knitting needles with a vengeance, producing socks and blankets for soldiers and evacuees, whilst countless jumble sales, beetle drives and concerts were organised to raise money for the War Effort.

Plans to safeguard the nation's children from enemy bombs were swiftly put into action and the massive evacuation from the densely populated areas began. A Hay resident since the war, Mrs Olive Grainger, was personally involved and has vivid memories of those traumatic days. In 1940 she was teaching in a school in the Elephant and Castle district of London when she and other teachers were ordered to accompany six hundred children who were to be evacuated first to an assessment centre at Seaford and from there consigned to various places of relative safety in the countryside.

She is still moved when she remembers the first stage of that dreadful journey. The walk from the school to London Bridge was about a mile and a half. The streets were empty of traffic but the pavements were lined with adults who were to remain in the city. Most stood in complete silence, many in tears, as they watched the children file past, but some distraught mothers, unable to control their anguish, ran behind, reaching for the children they thought they might never see again. Men came quietly from the crowd and walked alongside the smallest children, carrying their rucksacks and cases. Every child had been issued with a rucksack, inside which was a tin of corned beef, a tin of condensed milk, biscuits and chocolate and in their cases they carried a few spare clothes. Across each child's chest hung a rectangular cardboard box containing a gas-mask. Attached to the box was an identity card on which was written the child's name. The subsequent journey from the reception centre at Seaford to Hay was extremely harrowing as the train was packed with hundreds of frightened children from a number of city schools. Many of the younger children, unable to understand what was happening to them and badly missing their mothers, cried continually and clung to the few adults in charge for comfort. The journey seemed endless for the train kept stopping to drop off groups of children at small towns and villages along the way.

When the teacher and her charges reached Hay they found that a great effort had been made by the local residents to make them welcome. About 200 children had been allocated to the town and several cars were waiting at the railway station to transport them in relays to the Voluntary Infants' School, now the Parish Hall, in Lion Street. It was here that a group of kindly ladies, having set out the trestle tables, provided a meal for the hungry children and with smiles and cuddles they tried to comfort the tired and tearful youngsters as best they could.

The billeting officer organised the allocation of the children to various households. The majority of families took two children but some took as many as three or four even though money, space and provisions were in short supply. The local Council helped by distributing a stock of camp beds, blankets and pillows that had been donated by local families.

The people of Hay did their best to make the children feel part of their families and most of the youngsters settled down surprisingly quickly. Although the majority had only known life in the city they soon became accustomed to country ways and found that they enjoyed the novelty of their new surroundings—the farm animals being a special attraction.

Extra classes were set up to accommodate the evacuee children, one in the Infants' School in Lion Street and the other in the school on the Brecon Road. At four o'clock each day the teachers would take them down to the river where they would spend their time paddling with the local children until it was time to return to their billets for tea. Some of the boys managed to find work on the farms in their spare time and enjoyed it so much they were sorry to go home when the war ended. A number of them returned to Hay many times in the years that followed.

Life during the war years was, for most people, one of hardship and restriction. Ration books had been issued and these small, buff-coloured booklets began to dominate people's lives. Each page was divided into square coupons and the rough paper still retained little splinters of wood. Throughout Britain people were having to make do on 2 ounces of butter, meat and cheese per week and one egg. People in Hay were, however, more fortunate than those living in the cities. Additional fresh food—locally grown vegetables, milk, butter and eggs—was fairly plentiful, and that unpalatable stand-by, powdered egg in tins, although available in Hay, was seldom needed. Although sugar was also subject to rationing there was a concession for people who kept bees with the result that a number of hastily constructed hives started to appear overnight in back gardens.

There were two luxuries, however, that could not be bought, even on the Black Market—oranges and bananas. Some children had never tasted either until they were first given them by American soldiers who were lucky enough to receive food parcels from home. Eric Pugh remembers being the envy of his friends at school when he was given a banana for the first time by a local lad on leave from the Merchant Navy.

Petrol was also strictly rationed and as priority was given to service vehicles there was little for personal use. Not that many people in Hay had cars, relying instead on the railway. There were four trains a day between Hay and Hereford and the fare was 2 shilllings for a day return. A pony and trap could also be hired for country jaunts at a fairly low cost.

The markets continued as before, though the farmers were also subject to restrictions. A certain amount of meat, for instance, had to be transported to city areas and there were strict controls on the slaughter of animals for personal consumption. A Ministry official was appointed to snoop on people and report anyone killing a pig. The inspector was detested by many and a highly imaginative tale is told of the time he was spotted heading for a remote hill farm where the farmer had just finished killing one of his pigs. The family was thrown into a panic as he approached the front door. It was decided to drag the dead pig upstairs, wrap it in a blanket and hide it in the bed. The inspector, his suspicions aroused, entered the bedroom and was told that the ungainly lump under the eiderdown was that of the grandfather, ill with mumps. Hearing this, and fearing the consequences were he to become infected, the man from the Ministry turned tail and left and never bothered them again.

Soon after Dunkirk British troops were brought to Hay and some were billeted in the building in High Town that is now the Post Office. Many local families offered to take them in, provide them with meals or organise their laundry. A canteen for wounded soldiers was held every Sunday and many people opened their homes to servicemen for afternoon tea. It is said that some of the men still had sand from the beaches of France in their shoes. Mrs Betty Jones, for many years Hay's librarian, was only a young girl at the time but she remembers keeping some of the sand in a match-box as a curiosity. The men were, in general, very glad to find temporary accommodation and, on arrival, their first priority was usually a hot bath.

The people of Hay, like those everywhere, showed remarkable resilience to the tensions and privations of war—but they were fortunate for the only case of anyone coming under enemy fire resulted from a failure to comply with the black-out regulations. Eric Pugh remembers the Sunday morning when his father took him up to Cock-a-Lofty, an isolated cottage close to the foot of Hay Bluff. It seemed to him that the whole population of Hay was heading up the mountain road that morning to see the damage.

It transpired that the elderly woman living there, known as 'Lizzie Cock-a-Lofty', had forgotten to put up her black-out curtains the night before and the light from her oil-lamp had attracted an enemy aircraft which was on a bombing mission over Swansea. It was being chased by two Spitfires and the pilot, anxious to escape, off-loaded some incendiary bombs, one of which hit Cock-a-Lofty. Lizzie was lucky to escape injury and local lads gawped at the crater and rummaged amongst the debris looking for fragments of the incendiaries as souvenirs.

Restricted by the nightly black-out people tended to remain indoors as much as possible but regular dances were held, either at the Drill Hall, now Edward Foreman's Book Warehouse, The Swan Hotel or the Parish Hall. Some of the more mature ladies of Hay enjoyed dancing to a talented quintet led by Mr Rhys Harding, the local church organist and choir master. They were very popular, playing music in the Palm Court style and charged £5 a night for their services. But youngsters like Gladys Morgan and her friends preferred dancing to the American Service bands which were much more lively and played in the style of Glen Miller and the great swing bands of the time.

For those not keen on dancing there was the Plaza Cinema, showing two films a week—three, after War was declared. The original Plaza was little more than a corrugated hut at the back of J.V. Like's Garage—now removed to Three Cocks—built and managed by Desmond 'Dessie' Madigan, assisted by his brother, Mickey. Most of the films were 'weepies and war epics' although musicals were sometimes shown transporting the audience into another world by the dancing of Ginger Rogers and Fred Astaire. It was very popular. The cheapest seats were 6 pence—wooden benches covered with imitation leather, either to one side of the room so the image on the flickering screen was distorted, or so close to the front that one's ears were blasted by the crackling sound track. One shilling and three pence bought a seat further back which was red plush and much more comfortable. Tickets could be bought from Mrs Madigan at the family's bicycle shop at the end of Castle Street, now Brin Jenkins's Countrywear Clothes and Denys Parry's Gift Shop. The cinema had, of course, the requisite pea-souper fug of cigarette smoke and, more often than not, as in most picture houses at the time, the projector would fail—always, it seemed, at the most dramatic moment in the film, during a heart-rending death scene or a steamy clinch. This invariably meant an interval of several minutes during which some of the audience would happily hiss and cat-call until the spool was repaired whilst others would make a dash for the lavatories. If the break in transmission was expected to be

particularly long the management would play Bing Crosby records to enter-
tain the audience and keep them mellow. The new Plaza Cinema (now the Hay
Cinema Bookshop) was rebuilt on a much grander scale, but with the advent
of television the numbers of customers dwindled and, after being used for
some time as a venue for Saturday night dances, it was finally closed in 1957.

During the war there was a small electrical appliance factory called the
Little Atom at the back of Market Street (now Chattel's) where Mr Bondy had
once conducted his rabbit-skinning business. It was here that the notorious
killer, Donald Hume, was working during the war years. In 1948 he married
Cynthia, who, it is said, had been raised in Hay, but as she refused to leave
London and return to the town, he joined her in Finchley Road, near Golders
Green. It was here, a year later, that he committed his first murder, that of
Stanley Setty, a wealthy marketeer and car dealer. After stabbing him repeat-
edly with a German SS dagger (the motive may have been money but Setty
had recently infuriated Hume by kicking his beloved German Shepherd dog,
Tony), he dismembered the body with a hack-saw. He then hired a light
aircraft from Elstree Airport (where he had recently earned his licence to fly)
and, making two trips, threw the pieces into the English Channel. Tried at the
Old Bailey in January, 1950, Hume was sentenced to 12 years' imprisonment

Donald Hume under arrest after his Zurich bank raid

in Dartmoor, during which, because of his interest in electrical gadgets, he acquired the nick-name The Fuse.

Released in 1958 he departed for Switzerland and, adopting a number of aliases, resumed his criminal ways. In June of that year he published his 'Confession' in the *Sunday Pictorial* and twice returned to England to carry out an armed robbery on a Midland Bank in Brentford, West London. A year later, whilst attempting to escape after a bank robbery in Zurich, he killed for the second time, shooting a taxi-driver, Arthur Maag. For this he was sentenced to life imprisonment with hard labour. Brought back to England in 1976 he was sent to Broadmoor before being transferred to a psychiatric hospital in 1988. During his chequered life he patented the Little Atom Electric Toaster, named after his factory in Hay—which, it is said, he set fire to several times for the insurance money—and later penned a gangster novel entitled *The Dead Stay Dumb*.

Towards the end of the war a number of American servicemen, mainly officers, were billeted at The Moor, a large house on the Herefordshire outskirts of Hay, belonging to members of the Pennoyre family. The house was demolished in the early 1950s and only the walled garden and a picturesque tower remain. Generally speaking, the troops were made welcome in Hay—the black American serviceman causing a certain amount of curiosity—and although there were a number of fights in the local pubs most of the quarrels seemed to have arisen between the servicemen themselves. A number of Italian prisoners of war and Polish 'misplaced persons' were brought to Hay and put to work in the saw-mills in Potters Lane where special temporary huts were erected to house them. At the end of the war, as the gradual process of repatriation began, many of these men were replaced by German PoWs. The Italians PoWs worked mainly on local farms, picking potatoes, and if a farmer was unable to accommodate the prisoners himself, he would pay for them to be billeted with local families.

Not surprisingly, Hay was a scene of some fairly riotous behaviour on VE night, May 8, 1945. There was a large street party, mainly for women and children, in Chancery Lane (the old Pig Lane) with rows of trestle tables stretching from Broad Street to Brook Street and bunting strung from one side of the street to the other. Scores of people came out to celebrate that day and later in the evening, as more alcohol was consumed and the mood became even more exuberant, a tar-barrel was lit and rolled around the streets—reminiscent of the riotous Guy Fawkes celebrations of 1869. A large crowd gathered outside The Crown Hotel in Broad Street where some of the servicemen

Chancery Lane (formerly Pig Lane), once site of the pig market and later of VE day celebrations, demolished in 1974

were billeted. A group of local lads broke into the building and, encouraged by the cheers and high-spirits of the onlookers, hung the mattresses out of the top windows, ripping them open and shaking the feathers onto the crowds below. It is said that feathers could be seen floating about in Hay for several days after the celebrations.

The war was over at last, the troops were gone and life returned to the way it was and the dreary greyness of the post war years began.

CHAPTER 9

Town of Books

The post war years witnessed a slow decline in the fortunes of many small towns like Hay. As more people acquired cars, enabling them to travel further afield for a wider range of goods, the shops that were once vital to the community were no longer needed and the dependence on local trades was lost. Although the Thursday markets and sales of livestock continued as before, small businesses were closing down unable to compete with the city-based firms and no new industry was being established. As a result the young people, finding little opportunity for employment other than on the land, began to leave in search of more congenial and lucrative work elsewhere.

By the late Fifties Hay had reached a depressingly low point with much of its prosperity and innate optimism a thing of the past. Even more so when, in 1963, Dr Beeching completed his closure of the smaller and commercially less viable routes on the railway system so vital to rural communities, the Hereford-Hay-Brecon line, which had served the town for nearly a hundred years, being one of them. The station in Newport Street closed after the arrival of the last train on 31 December, 1962. Mr Maurice John, the station-master, recalls the headlights of the train coming into view and the driver, having built up a good head of steam, released a billowing cloud of smoke that ran the length of the train. The whistle, he remembers 'set up a continuous shriek' and, having commandeered some detonators to mark the momentous occasion, these were exploded 'in quick succession, each one giving a vivid flash while the train drew in to the tumultuous cheers of the children aboard.'

A house close to the site of the old railway station—now the premises of the Hay and Brecon Farmers Co-operative—still bears the inscription Station

*Boz Books (with window awning) the site of the old Fire Station and, under
Richard Booth, the first of the current plethora of second hand bookshops*

Stores. To many, inhabitants and visitors alike, the railway is still sadly missed
and its passing truly marked the end of an era.

But Hay did not sink into isolation. Instead the whole economy of the town
was about to change and it was mainly due to the inhabitants' ability to adapt
to this change that ensured its survival.

The man responsible for Hay's most recent revival is Richard Booth. In
1962, when he was 23, he bought a small shop for £700. It was originally the
old Fire Station (now Boz Books) in Church Street, opposite the Blue Boar,
commemorated by an old fireman's helmet hanging high on a hook on the
front wall. This seemingly unimportant transaction marked the beginning of a
remarkable metamorphosis, that of a small market town into the largest
trading centre for second-hand and out-of-print books in the world. Trading
had once more become the life blood of the town only this time the
commodity for sale was not beef, corn or wool but books.

Although a number of booksellers have become established in Hay in the
wake of this innovation, Richard Booth has become synonymous with the
Town of Books. This is largely due to the outrageous events and publicity-
seeking gimmicks he staged in his early years in the book business, much to
the irritation of some local people and the jubilation of others. And it worked.
Reporters and film crew flocked to the town with notebooks and pencils

poised, confident of good copy. *The Independent* has described him as 'a deceptively vague and rumpled man' and *Private Eye* as 'an idealist and self-publicist, jousting with authority'.

Richard Booth comes from a military family, related on his mother's side to William Pitt the Younger. In 1960 his father, Colonel Philip Booth, retired to Brynmelin, a late Victorian house in Cusop Dingle, a mile from the town. He brought with him his wife, three daughters and Richard. Born in 1938, the latter had endured a fairly miserable but orthodox upper class education; his most vivid memory of his post war junior school was being given dreadful meals of spam and warm lettuce. At another school boys had to suffer a master who refused the rectify his failing eye-sight by wearing glasses, relying instead on his 'ultra-sensitive hearing to rush like a blind pig on punitive missions'. Once the miscreant was within his grasp he would viciously twist the hair at the back of the neck to give full vent to his displeasure.

Rugby School followed, then Oxford to read history though Richard admits to spending an inordinate amount of time hanging around St Clare's, an English Language School. He and another undergraduate found having a car a great advantage and many hours were spent, not in study, but in 'drinking and going out with foreign girls'.

On leaving Oxford family pressure steered him towards a business career but after an abortive attempt at becoming an accountant, a field in which he had neither aptitude nor interest, he turned his attention to antiques. Several maverick excursions into the world of antiques proved less than successful and Richard was once more presented with the problem faced by many graduates—how was he to earn a living with only a history degree and a character that was autonomous, innovative and distinctly anarchistic?

Buying the old Fire Station and filling it with books seemed as good a solution as any. He scoured the country in search of as many books as he could lay his hands on, sometimes buying the contents of whole bookshops and even a number of complete libraries originally belonging to Welsh Working Men's Clubs. In Ireland he bought an entire library of books that had been undisturbed for two hundred years and he recalls that some of the volumes were so thick with dust that handling them was like 'touching the fur of a young rabbit'.

Due to the depressed economy in Hay at the time, premises were readily available and relatively cheap. As many of the shops were lying empty, lending Hay an air of dereliction, buying floor space to accommodate the growing mountain of books presented no problem. There was also a local workforce prepared to do all the heavy lifting, sorting and travelling necessary in return for relatively low wages.

Booth's vision of a second-hand book empire focused on a need for vast numbers of out-of-print books, hitherto inaccessible but now gathered together in one place. 'Old books never die', he has always maintained and insists that 'no matter how unattractive a book may be to 99% of the people there is always somebody, somewhere, who wants it'. His method also afforded a library or university the chance to buy a large number of titles on one subject, no matter how obscure.

One of the biggest problems was building all the book shelves. The solution, however, was a man named Frank English. In his recently published autobiography, *My Kingdom of Books*, Richard recalls his first sighting of Frank in the kitchen at Brynmelin drinking a mug of tea with 'cigarette smoke curled around a large, beak-like, magenta nose. Thin legs were twisted into a spiral and anchored to the floor by a pair of old Army boots.' He was described by Paul Minet in his book, *Late Booking*, as 'an anarchist, bookman, carpenter, talker, spendthrift, yet a boon companion and charmer.' He was all of these and one of Hay's more memorable characters.

How he and Richard first formed what was to be a long and volatile alliance is a story often told. Frank, who was working as a gardener for Richard's parents at the time, in the throes of some aberration—for he was not the marrying kind—took it into his head to propose to a local licensee (rumour has it the lady was the legendary Lucy Powell, licensee of The Three Tuns to whom he proposed quite regularly) and, on being refused, proceeded to become so paralytically drunk that he had to be transported back to Brynmelin in a taxi. This was the last straw as far as Richard's mother was concerned— Frank, an inveterate chain-smoker, was also apt to set fire to his bed—and she sacked him. Richard, however, felt suitably inspired to take him on and, in the years that followed, as Paul Minet aptly remarks, Frank 'must have built miles of bookcases, staircases and even complete floors for Richard in the intervals of being rescued from scandal, from debt and from ditches'. Despite his excesses Frank lived to reach his late seventies but died in 1992 of throat cancer, sadly missed by many who knew him well.

Initially, the rewards of the second-hand book business were good. In 1963 Richard bought Hay Castle from Victor Tuson, who had married into the prosperous Studt fairground family, owners of the piers at Aberystwyth and Llandudno. So it was that when Richard took over the castle it still housed various defunct fairground artefacts, 'twisted golden pillars from the carousel and a horse with a chipped mane and peeling red nostrils'. The interior, however, was in good condition with wonderful oak floors, panelled rooms and four-poster beds though much of the huge Jacobean staircase had been destroyed in a fire in 1939.

In 1968, Richard married for the first time, a young lady called Elizabeth Westoll, but the marriage only lasted a year. By this time the annual turnover of his book business had reached £100,000 and, as a mark of his success, Richard bought a Phantom V Rolls Royce to grace the Castle drive and proceeded to adopt a life-style to match. Much of the publicity surrounding him in this period has been exaggerated and become part of the Sixties' myth that life was one long party. Indeed, there were parties during the Sixties and Seventies—Marianne Faithful and the late Henrietta Moraes being among the glamourous visitors from London—and some of them rather wild, but it was also a period when Richard and his colleagues approached the business of book-dealing with tremendous energy and enthusiasm and, in true Hay tradition, some serious drinking sessions.

Richard's favourite drinking hole at the time was The Masons' Arms, now a SPAR foodstore, (the original licence was granted before 1776 and expired in 1971) which was run by an incredibly tolerant couple, Ken and Violet Jenkins. In the early days Richard and his entourage, which always included a number of hangers-on eager to take advantage of his generosity, were there most nights, sometimes still drinking at four in the morning. Until that is, Richard decided to leave, as often as not staggering along the passage towards the castle, giggling helplessly like some latter-day Toad.

Great schemes were hatched within the thick, nicotine-coated walls of The Masons' Arms and within a few years Richard was travelling regularly throughout the British Isles and Ireland in his search for books. He was soon making frequent trips to America where he filled huge containers with as many as 15,000 books at a time. These were then sent over to be sorted, priced and sold in Hay, very often to tourists from the self-same American cities from whence the books had come.

The business was expanding rapidly. In 1969 Richard bought Mr Madigan's redundant Plaza Cinema, and set Frank English the colossal task of shelving it throughout. He also opened a number of specialist shops in the town stocking books on medicine, erotica, topography, natural history, periodicals and one consisting only of prints.

By the mid-Seventies Richard had a staff of twenty and a million books and was listed in the *Guinness Book of Records* for having more second-hand books and more miles of shelving than anyone else in the world. One venture, however, that proved less than successful was the acquisition of Cockcroft House, formerly the old Union Workshouse. Here Richard amassed a vast collection of Americana, no less than 20,000 books and thousands more on theology. Though still, at that time, a rather cold and gloomy place, it was here that Rev Ian Paisley would come to browse in the Theology section under the watchful eyes of his minders, surprisingly, perhaps, in absolute silence.

That same year Richard made a disastrous but brief second marriage, this time to a Spanish girl, Victoria del Rio, an episode around which has grown, as with everything he does, a wealth of speculative rumour.

It was on 1 April, 1977, that one of Richard's more ambitious schemes reached fruition when he declared Hay an independent kingdom, appointing himself, of course, as king—King Richard, Coeur du Livres. He made an inspired speech of inauguration in the face of some good-natured heckling from his bemused subjects, some of whom had assembled in polite groups in the castle grounds to hear the proclamation.

Little wonder that April Ashley, another flamboyant and abrasive character, formerly merchant seaman, George Jameson, much-loved by the media, found herself drawn, for a while at least, to Richard and life in Hay. Always looking glamorous and beautifully turned out she not only acted for a time as his official consort but also contributed to an entertaining Booth broadsheet called *The Hay Herald*, as a successful agony aunt to both sexes. In 1985, she left the town, heading for San Diego, depositing her autistic whippet, Florabelle, in Bear Street with her friend, Molly, and, with a last imperious wave of her hand she was gone.

Throughout Richard's proclamation speech the Hay Air Force, a solitary two-seater Beagle, circled overhead, under orders from April, the newly appointed Duchess of Offa's Dyke, to dip its wings every time it passed over her house. The National Anthem for Independent Hay was an imaginative rendering of Colonel Bogey and the town's navy consisted of a two-man rowing dingy on the River Wye. Richard's crown was a makeshift, glue and glass affair trimmed with cotton wool 'ermine' and the orb was a ball-cock dipped in a bucket of gold paint. Some years later it was rumoured that both these relics had been secreted from the castle and subsequently found on a train half-way to Merthyr after Richard had thrown a party for 800 striking miners from the Valleys.

Having declared Independence, a challenge fired by his 'burning resentment of the damage done to the town by fifty years of council and government

108

bureaucracy' the newly crowned monarch was willing to bestow various titles for money, and gullible would-be aristocrats happily exchanged hard currency for a fake earldom at £15, a knighthood at £2.50 or a dukedom at £25, whilst Hay passports were on sale for 75p a piece.

April Ashley, one time official consort of 'King' Richard Booth, posing outside Mr Mayall's shop

It was brilliant publicity and it worked. Three television stations and eight national newspapers covered the 'Home Rule for Hay' celebrations and to set the seal on this frankly surreal event the king renamed his horse Caligula and made him Prime Minister. The publicity brought thousands more visitors to Hay and the press continued to arrive in search of Richard who, as Paul Minet states in his book had 'moved from the occasional piece of copy into that of a minor celebrity, the best known second-hand bookseller in Britain and a famous eccentric'.

Eccentric he most certainly is, though he would deny it, but his irate diatribes against the manner in which big business, the press barons, the tourist industry and bureaucracy in general spends millions of pounds a year on the destruction of rural communities have always maintained a central core of truth. His early vision of a rural revival was dismissed by many as being idealistic clap-trap, yet the sentiments he expressed which seemed *avant garde* or nonsensical then, are now echoed by a number of environmental groups and local government

Richard Booth with regalia,
astride his horse, Goldie

departments—notably those of a resurgence of rural self-sufficiency and a gradual return to traditional crafts.

It may be that the thrust of his argument was lost by the sale of T-shirts bearing messages like Balls to Walls or Father Died of Mother's Pride. These provocative gestures certainly attracted attention but possibly detracted from the serious issues being addressed, though the idea of an astute man of vision playing the fool to make a serious point is by no means new. It must be said, however, that his message was somewhat diluted on one occasion when, in full throttle about the supremacy of the horse as a means of travel he paused mid-sentence to tell one of his men to go and get the car ready for the next buying trip. Likewise, there were some rueful smiles when, at the time he was proclaiming the evils of mass-produced food, his housekeeper could be seen regularly descending the steps of the local supermarket, carrier bags bulging with provisions for the king. His staff have had to cope with similar inconsistencies over the years. On many occasions a minion has worked diligently, often in freezing conditions, to compile a collection, perhaps with a buyer in mind, only to find the best volumes sold overnight to buy petrol the following day.

Disaster struck, however, in November 1977 when the Jacobean part of Hay Castle was damaged by fire and lay, once more, in ruins. Unfortunately, a number of rare books also went up in flames. The more uncharitable nursed suspicions that the blazing log that rolled from the grate that night was somehow miraculously propelled by prayers of supplication and the prospect of the insurance money being used to bale out a bookselling business that was in decline. Those who know Richard, however, know better, for no matter how many other reprehensible deeds may have been laid at his door over the years this is not one of them. The castle is too important to him, on a number of levels, and his affinity with the building rules out any such act of vandalism.

Anxious to repair the devastating damage caused by the fire using master craftsmen and, as far as possible, traditional methods, Richard made the acquaintance of Roger Capps, a charismatic young man from South Wales and an inspired builder with a passion for the repair of old buildings. Having assessed the extent of the damage which, in fact, had removed some of the later restorations to reveal the Jacobean structure including many original details, Capps moved into the few remaining, but barely habitable, rooms in the castle and set up his masonry and timber workshops in the grounds.

For a time Booth and Capps shared a messianic commitment to the restoration of the castle and a compulsion to risk their necks on horseback, Kamikaze-style, down the sides of mountains. However, in 1982, following a volatile breach, Capps's involvement with Hay Castle, for a while at least, came to an end. Sadly unable to complete the repairs as planned he removed to Llowes Court, thrown, as it were, from the castle like Maud's stone. From their new base Capps and his team of craftsmen continue to work on many of the finest buildings in the Marches, including Hereford Cathedral, Goodrich Castle, Wigmore Castle and, after the calamitous fire of November, 1992, they replaced the massive timber roof of St George's Hall, Windsor Castle, the largest green oak structure since the 16th century. More recently, Capps and his company, on behalf of UNESCO, has been involved in the repair of some of the most important mosques and monuments in Central Asia, including two mausolea in Uzbekistan—the Bayan Khuli Khan and the 10th century Ismail Sumani—a Hanseatic warehouse in Latvia and a monastery in Romania, training and supervising the local workforce in the most appropriate methods of consolidation and repair.

As for Richard Booth, he now sells antiquarian books from the Castle, the remaining restoration having been completed by Stansells, renowned for their repair work on Wells Cathedral. The distinctive Elizabethan chimneys have been rebuilt each involving the replacement of 7,000 hand-made bricks. He still owns The Limited in Lion Street, reputed to be one of the largest bookshops in the world. He and his third wife, Hope, have opened a bookshop in Montolieu, Southern France, and continue to be involved in many other book-towns, similar to Hay in concept, that have been set up throughout the world. The town of Hay is twinned with that of Redu-Libin, in Belgium.

In 1995, Booth survived an operation to remove a benign brain tumour which has left him with some paralysis on his left side. He continues, however, to expound his ideologies and develop his book-selling business, even venturing into selling through the Internet.

But what of Hay, the town of books he did so much to revitalise forty years ago? The whole ambience of the place has, inevitably, been altered by the influx of visitors drawn to the town primarily for the books. This in turn has provided the opportunity for a number of other booksellers—at least thirty-six at the time of writing—many of whom once worked for Richard Booth, to take advantage of Hay's reputation and world wide clientele to set up on their own. The first was the respected bookseller, Michael 'Chalkie' White who worked from a shop in Market Street and, twenty years ago, Diana Blunt established Pemberton's Bookshop, offering readers access to an wide range of new books. It is appropriate, perhaps, for a town of books, that the mayor for 1999 was Karl Showler, well-known for his writings on, amongst other genre, his specialist subject, bees. Author of *The Observation Hive*, he also contributes to the English Language Bee Press, The Kilvert Society newsletter and has a regular column in *Bee Craft*.

Lacking any central park or municipal gardens the inhabitants of Hay tend to use the river banks as places of recreation, though in the 1920s Hay Common, with its original Golf Course (the present one is at Summerhill, between Hay and Clifford) was popular for walks and picnics. Whilst some enjoy walking the Begwyns, Hay Bluff or the Brecon Beacons, closer to Hay the favourite areas are Bailey's Walk and a 19-acre riverside meadow on the south bank of the Wye called The Warren. In 1962, The Warren Club managed to raise enough money to purchase the land as a protected place for the people of Hay to enjoy. It is managed by a committee of Trustees and it was written into the deeds of purchase that the land could never be sold for property development or commercial use.

Hay Wire, an irreverently entertaining local rag edited by Richard Moule, alias 'Dickie Moonshine', has now taken the place of *The Hay Herald*, and provides an insight into the social history of Hay, past and present.

In addition to the plethora of bookshops in the town, Y Gelli Book Auctions and the usual grocery, butcher's and clothing outlets, there are a number of antique shops, several craft units, an Oriental carpet shop, Mr Lee's Chinese Take-Away and shops specialising in Jigsaw Puzzles and

Teddy Bears. Several painters and potters are at work in the area, some of whom regularly sell their work in the Made in Hay bazaar held in May and December each year. Within Hay there are three galleries, The Globe, (formerly the United Reform Church on the corner of Newport Street and Heol-y-dwr), Rogue's Gallery, in Broad Street and The Hay Makers, close to St John's Chapel, between Lion Street and the Bull Ring. In Clyro, two miles from Hay, there is The Kilvert Gallery, Ashbrook House, formerly the home of Francis Kilvert, where Liz Organ and Eugene Fisk, both artists, hold excellent, occasionally eclectic, exhibitions of painting and sculpture on a regular basis.

In place of the small independent schools that have served the town at various times in the past there is now a single state school—Hay Primary School—situated close to the main car park, currently with 150 pupils on the roll.

During the summer months, when Hay is teeming with visitors, the Town Crier, Ken Smith, resplendent in his official regalia of gold-braided, crimson coat, hose, buckled shoes and black three-cornered hat, springs into action, ringing his bell and, in fine voice, calls out the traditional 'Oyez! Oyez! Oyez!' before announcing forthcoming events to groups of bemused, and at times uncomprehending, visitors.

The twice yearly fairs continue in May and November: so, too, the live-stock sales, the Thursday markets and the annual Hay Horse and Pony Show, which is held each spring. The Three Cocks Vintage Society hold their annual show at Boatside Farm in August each year, one of the main attractions being the display of traction engines which are meticulously maintained by, amongst others, T.S. Henderson and F.J. Williams & Sons, Builders' Merchants, of Newport Street.

The three-day Raft Race on the River Wye, starting at Hay Bridge and ending at Chepstow, is held in May each year, with up to fifty craft taking part. Established more than 20 years ago, sponsors of this event, which attracts competitors world-wide, have raised large amounts of money for charity.

In Hay, as anywhere else, history has shown that empires are built and empires fall and whilst one business may flourish, another might fail ensuring that the history of this small community is forever changing. The largest employer in Hay at present is Leon Morelli, a London businessman who came to the town in the early Eighties. Initially, his acquisition of a number of properties was seen by many as a challenge to the King of Hay's position as the mainstay of the town's economy. This perceived rivalry, however unfounded, has rumbled on for years, at times descending into farce, and, of course, readily fuelled by the press. His arrival corresponded with a time when Richard Booth Booksellers, after a period of prosperity in the Sixties and Seventies, was nearing bankruptcy. In 1982, Morelli's Pharos Group of Companies purchased the Hay Cinema Bookshop from Richard Booth and subsequently acquired a number of other venues in the town, including The Kilvert Country Hotel. It also owns Brecon Pharmaceuticals Ltd, a hi-tech packaging operation, known locally as the 'Pill Factory', with premises on Forest Road and at the Wye Valley Business Park on Brecon Road and currently employing more than 100 people. The Pharos Group has contributed financially to a number of local concerns including the Black Mountain Lions, the sports field and the Information Technology Centre at Hay Primary School. It also sponsored the Hay Festival of Literature in its early years and the Brecon Jazz Festival.

Undoubtedly, many people of Hay have benefited from the increase in tourism in the area, the innkeepers, the shopkeepers, the café proprietors and the Bed & Breakfast establishments. The knock-on effect of these businesses and others involved in leisure activities is that they can offer employment to many of the younger generation of Hay residents who have chosen to remain in the town rather than seek work further afield. This has resulted in an unusual and healthy mix of ages and interests within such a small community of, according to the last census in 1991, only 1,407 inhabitants.

The growing popularity of Hay and the continued press coverage has resulted in the establishment of the annual Hay Festival of Literature, first introduced by the late Norman Florence in 1988, and now under the direction of his son, Peter Florence. It has been described by the *New York Times* as 'one of the most important Festivals in the English-speaking world', by *The Guardian* as 'a literary Smorgasbord' and by *The Times* as 'the British Bayreuth'. This prestigious event is currently sponsored by, amongst others, *The Sunday Times*, Carlton UK Television, BBC 2 Network Television and BBC Radios 2, 3 and 4, Channel 4, Classic FM, The Elmley Foundation, *The New Yorker*, *The Times Literary Supplement*, *Esquire Magazine* and *The Western Mail* and more than 40 local businesses. It is also funded by The Arts Council of Wales and attracts more than 35,000 visitors each year eager to attend performances by many high-profile, world-class writers, several of whom have been Nobel Prize winners, as well as musicians, both classical and pop, alternative stand-up comics, poets and popular media personalities.

As a quite separate entity, a Hay Childrens Festival of the Arts, under the direction of Caroline Wylie, runs for several days during the Festival of Literature, providing a programme of creatve activities especially devised for 6-12 year olds, featuring authors, poets, illustrators and performance artists.

For several years an annual Halloween extravaganza, Hay-on-Fire, was staged at various venues in the town, a popular event that attracted a large following. Founded and directed by 'Goffeee' (David Goff Eveleigh), it featured a torch-light procession and spectacular fire theatre, massed fire performers, giant puppets, fire labyrinths, wicker giants, fire sculptures on land and water, fireworks, traction engines and music and dance. 'Goffeee' was also responsible for Hay's National Circus and Theatre Convention, another annual event held as close to April Fool's Day as possible, which ran for 10 years at both Hay Castle and Clyro Court—it comprised a week long programme of workshops devoted to the circus arts and culminated in a weekend of impromptu performances through the streets of Hay.

Had Francis Kilvert been able, even for one moment, to imagine an influx of thousands of visitors to Hay each year—not only the bibliophiles but also the hill-walkers, the canoeists, the hang-gliders and the pony-trekkers—he would have been appalled. On Tuesday 5 April, 1870, he went to see progress on the building of Father Ignatius's monastery at Capel-y-Ffyn in the Black Mountains and from there to see the ruins of Llanthony Priory. During this visit he met *two* visitors which so angered him that this normally tolerant and compassionate man felt moved to write this uncharacteristically harsh tirade in his diary:

> ... What was our horror on entering the enclosure to see two tourists with staves and shoulder belts all complete postured among the ruins in an attitude of admiration, one of them of course discoursing learnedly to his gaping companion and pointing out objects of interest with his stick. If there is one thing more hateful than another it is being told what to admire and having objects pointed out to one with a stick. Of all noxious animals too the most noxious is a tourist. And of all tourists the most vulgar, illbred, offensive and loathesome is the British tourist.

What, one wonders, would he have made of the many thousands who, having enjoyed reading his Diary, come to pay homage to him and to the glorious countryside that so inspired him?

Bibliography

Beales, Martin *Dead Not Buried*, Robert Hale, 1995

Booth, Richard and Stuart, Lucia *My Kingdom in Books*, Y Lolfa Cyf, 1999

Davies, D.J. (ed.) *The Place of Brecknock in the Industrialization of South Wales*, 1961

Fairs, Geoffrey L. *The History of The Hay*, Phillimore & Co, 1972
     Annals of A Parish: A Short History of Hay-on-Wye, 1994

Hay Parish Magazine, 1886

Hodges, Geoffrey *Owain Glyn Dwr and the War of Independence in the Welsh Border*, Logaston Press, 2000

Jones, Theophilus *History of Brecknockshire*, 1805

Lockwood, David *Francis Kilvert*, Seren Books, 1990
     Kilvert, The Victorian, Poetry Wales Press, 1992

Minet, Paul *Late Booking*, Frantic Press, 1989

Morris, Jan *The Matter of Wales: Epic Views of a Small Country*, OUP, 1984

Moule, Richard (ed.) *Hay Wire*

Odell,Robin , Gaute, Joe and Trumper, Dr. *Exhumation of a Murder*, Harrap, 1975

Remfry, Paul *Castles of Breconshire, Monuments in the Landscape Vol VIII*, Logaston Press, 1999

Thomas, Hugh *A History of Wales*, University of Wales Press, 1972

Plomer, William (ed.) *The Diary of Rev Francis Kilvert.*, Jonathan Cape, 1938

Richards, Mark *Through Welsh Border Country*, Thornhill Press, 1976

Smith, Eldon *Crime & Punishment in England and Wales*, Gomer Press, 1986

Stockinger, Victor *The Rivers Wye and Lugg Navigation*, Logaston Press, 1996

Victorian and Edwardian Crime, Batsford Ltd. 1978

Williams, Glanmor *History of Wales. Vol III. Recovery, Reorientation & Reformation: Wales c.1415-1642*, Clarendon Press/University of Wales Press 1987

Whittington-Egan, Richard and Molly *The Murder Almanac*, Neil Wilson Publishing, 1992

Wilson, Colin and Pitman, Patricia *Encyclopedia of Murder*, Pan, 1962

Young, Filson (ed.) 'The Trial of H R Armstrong' in *Notable British Trials*, James Hodge, 1927

Index